A TOWER IN A WALL

Dame Freya Stark, self-portrait, 1966

A Tower in a Wall

by

ALEXANDER MAITLAND

1804
William Blackwood
Edinburgh

First published in 1982 by
William Blackwood & Sons Ltd,
32 Thistle Street,
Edinburgh EH2 1HA

British Library Cataloguing in Publication Data

Maitland, Alexander
A tower in a wall : a portrait of Dame Freya Stark
1. Stark, Freya 2. Travellers, Biography
I. Title
910'.92'4 G246.S/

ISBN 0 – 85158 – 159 – 5

Printed by William Blackwood & Sons Ltd

To
Margaret

Contents

Introduction

We two stood simply friend-like side by side,
Viewing a twilight country far and wide. . . .

A BLUE *Siamic* single-decker bus carried us away from the suburbs of Treviso, through a dusty landscape of vineyards and shuttered villas, through a sprawl of little country towns, to Asolo, a miniature Renaissance city, fifty kilometres northwest of Venice, perched in the foothills of the Alps. As we approached along steepening winding roads, the afternoon sun pinpointed the Rocca, a ruined fortress which overlooks Asolo and marks its position from the plain. After travelling for about an hour, towards the mountains, the bus swung left and climbed abruptly between low stone parapets through the pinewood shade of the Nuovo Foresto; then, gathering speed at the crest of the hill, it swept round the colonnaded Via Roberto Browning, up into Asolo's main square. The driver, who had recognised me at the Treviso terminus, politely handed down my suitcase, muttered '*Arrivederci*' and nodded as a small figure in a duffle-coat, face shadowed by a wide-brimmed hat, advanced smiling, her arms outstretched in welcome. '*Eccoti, signore*,' said the driver, '*signora Stark!*'

Freya embraced me several times. 'Shall we go straight up to the tower? Everything's ready for you there. . . .'

The square was quiet. A few couples sat outside the café at wrought-iron tables set among evergreen shrubs in white barrels. Cars were parked haphazardly between the trees or ranged in front of a church and along the pavements. Near the fountain with its winged lion, a policeman in short sleeves touched his cap to Freya as we passed. The frescoed walls and barley-sugar grillework; the narrow, sloping streets and slitted alleyways; the blindish elevations of the houses; and the worn, uneven paving-stones, all served as eloquent reminders of Asolo's antiquity. I looked down between the church and school, across a terrace whose fringe of cypresses and palm-trees screened the plain which in the distance faded to the Euganean Hills and the Lagoon. Freya gestured with her stick: 'Verona . . . Vicenza . . . that way, Padua. I don't think I would like to live down there. Terribly flat countryside and, of course, in summer like an oven. Summers are sufficiently hot up here in our little town.'

'You of all people shouldn't mind the heat. It can't be anything like Arabia or Persia.'

'No, it isn't, in the actual number of degrees. But there you find a dry heat which is bearable; here it gets stuffy and uncomfortable. I mean, you know what London is like on a hot summer day. Really unpleasant: no wind, just that awful suffocating heat.'

We turned into the Via Belvedere, leading up towards the tower. Freya halted beneath a little plaque: 'This was put up by a merchant a long time ago; poor man had been involved in some scandal. . . . Can you read what it says? "*Signore; benedici chi s'interessa dei Fatti suoi* ('Lord, bless those who attend to their own business')." Apt, don't you think?'

We continued uphill, past terraced pink and blue stucco cottages, until we came to a pair of immense green street-doors set in an extension of the city wall. Inside, we walked past the house belonging to Caroly Piaser, who had been for many years secretary to Flora Stark, Freya's mother. Now signora Piaser kept an eye on Freya's affairs and managed the *tessoria*, a tiny silk-factory which Flora had once owned, on the corner of the Via Robert Browning. A flight of broad steps and an earth patio brought us at last to the tower; Freya unlocked the split-leaf double doors and pushed them wide open. Then she nodded towards a garden-table and chairs near by.

‘Let’s sit here in the sunshine and have tea. It’s so lovely this afternoon! Why not just leave your suitcase in the hall?’

Aconites, primroses and wild iris grew among the lush grass of the tower garden, whose terraces sloped down to the Via Canova where Freya lived in a sunny apartment filled with books. The patio faced south-east towards the Adriatic, looking through pomegranates and cypresses, over crinkled roofs of terracotta tiles. To the northwest lay Monte Grappa. On the hill directly above us, the Rocca’s battlements loomed in sunlight. Just above the main square, at the head of the Via Sottocastello, Queen Cornaro’s castle rose from massive foundations of natural rock.

* * * *

Queen Cornaro, or to be more precise, Caterina, Queen of Cyprus, Jerusalem and Armenia – a member of the powerful Cornaro family – settled at Asolo in 1488, after her defeat by the Venetians. The exiled monarch lived in the castle and also kept a house in Venice. Her courtiers accompanied her, and Asolo’s streets still consist of the gracious dwellings they built at that time. W.C. Hazlett recorded in *The Venetian Republic* that the Queen ‘was a short plump woman with a handsome countenance and sparkling eyes, of genial conversation, yet dignified in her manner’ who ‘spent the rest of her life in works of piety and benevolence, in cultivating her gardens and in the enjoyment of literary society’. It has been said that Hazlett over-romanticised the Queen’s biography; be that as it may, his words might as easily have described my remarkable companion.

After a lull of four hundred years, towards the end of the nineteenth century, the town emerged once more from peaceful obscurity, having been adopted and immortalised by Robert Browning. The association was commemorated by the winding street that bears his name, leading off the main piazza, and by a slim volume of poems entitled *Asolando*, first published in 1889.

Robert and Elizabeth Barrett Browning's only son, Pen, lived at Asolo for much of his life. He was stocky and often wore a straw boater, exaggerating his round, ruddy features which, Freya told me, as a child, reminded her of an orange. Pen Browning had a mania for buying and restoring old houses and once owned as many as four in Asolo, including an enormous villa, like a barracks, above the piazza close to the North Gate. Browning added a romantic tower music-room to another villa, visible from Queen Cornaro's castle, with four open sides and a balustrade running all round.

The little hilltop town, with its picturesque medieval charm, caught the imagination of late-Victorian painters and sculptors who visited it towards the end of the 1880s. Among them was an Australian artist-photographer called Herbert Young, who filled albums with sensitive studies of Asolo and the surrounding countryside; and Young's friend, Robert Stark, the son of a family of West Country landowners and cider-brewers, who had completed his training as a sculptor and painter in Paris. Stark fell in love immediately with everything he saw and rushed back to Paris to fetch his wife, Flora, a first cousin and herself an excellent painter and musician. The Starks rented a house at the Loreggia Gate and for some years commuted between Asolo and Montmartre.

Soon after 8 a.m., on Tuesday, 31st January 1893, the couple's first child, Freya Madeline, was born in Paris in their studio at 37 Rue Denfert Rochereau. The Starks' baby daughter had arrived two months prematurely; nevertheless, Flora described her as 'healthy, active, vigorous and good-tempered'. Sixteen months later, in Venice, Flora gave birth to a second child, Vera Joséphine, who died young after an unhappy marriage. Freya, aged thirteen, narrowly escaped being killed by an electric loom in the Piedmont silk-factory belonging to Count Mario Roascio, her future brother-in-law. She survived to become a famous Arabist, traveller and author; as Dame Freya Stark, she is now regarded as perhaps the twentieth century's most outstanding chronicler of Middle-East and Eastern-Mediterranean environments.

* * * *

I carried the tea-tray out to the garden, where Freya sat in her large brown felt hat with the squashy brim, admiring the view. She had unbuttoned her brown-and-white woollen duffel-coat which, she remarked, had been bought a few months previously in the bazaar at Khatmandu. Under the duffel-coat, she wore a moss-green woollen dress which she told me she found practical and, I discovered later, wore often, including in the evenings, if she decided not to change for dinner. The felt sombrero covered a close-fitting green silk cap, edged with black lace, and tied under her chin with black silk ribbons.

Freya used her hands as she talked. They were small and workmanlike, not the white, silken appendages of a Regency heroine, but rather the capable instruments of a sculptress or a nurse, with short, supple fingers, nails clipped to a point and the backs and wrists sunburned and speckled with grey sun-cancers. Her hands had the sort of well-travelled, well-worn appearance one associates with people who had spent the greater part of their lives out of doors, in the heat.

Standing erect, she reached a little over five feet in height. Seated, in a contemplative mood, she would often crouch, poised on the edge of her chair, her hands cupped one above the other, gently massaging the knuckles, while she considered a question or searched her imagination for precisely the right words to express an idea or conjure up some recollection from the past. She would spread herself comfortably under the folds of her long skirts and lean forward resting on her elbows. In this familiar posture, Freya would give a companion her undivided attention.

As we sat on the patio drinking tea, she would now and again wave away a fly with a little furtive movement; gently, however, as if she meant always to divert rather than destroy it. Sometimes, unconsciously, she would fiddle with one of her rings, or run a finger back and forth along the edge of the table. Or merely gesture.

At eighty-nine, she radiated warmth and humour and demonstrated the same forces of originality and intellect which had distinguished her conversation and writing for fifty years. Generally mellow, her voice would now and then run up and down in soprano cadences. Her eyes sparkled with vitality and her lightly powdered, somewhat Roman features, lent strength to the subtle polyglot inflections in her voice.

Freya Stark had lived a unique and varied life and continued to do so, having scarcely modified the range of her activities. In fact, about the only significant difference was that where, formerly, she had walked, she now rode; but she had used mules or ponies in any case for years in Syria and in the Eastern Highlands of Turkey.

Her most recent journey had been made in the Himalayan foothills of Western Nepal in 1981. Filmed by Colin Luke, who, four years previously, had directed a B.B.C. 2 television film of Freya's nostalgic voyage by raft down the Syrian Euphrates, this beautiful film of Freya's mountain odyssey contains reflective conversational pauses and shows her climbing on ponyback through forests and villages and along steep, dangerously narrow mountain trails.

When we had finished tea, Freya retrieved her walking-stick and handbag and stood up. 'Now, let's see that you're quite comfortable in your little fortress!'

The tower's outer doors stood welcomingly ajar. It was a three-storeyed building, roughly twenty feet square on plan, and consisted of an entrance-hall, from which a flight of wooden stairs led to a small kitchen extension off the half-landing; to a bedroom with a shower and lavatory, on the first-floor; and finally through a trapdoor to a big second-floor sitting-room, with sliding windows which ran the full length of three walls. There were small square windows with iron grilles, set deep in thick stonework, one on either side of the entrance. Twisted branches of creeper reached up to the squat masonry pillars dividing the sitting-room windows. Doves perched inquisitively on the overhanging eaves of Roman tile, and trees – cypress, lime and bay – growing on the patio above the rose-arbour darkened the bedroom in summer.

Two enormous barred and studded chests stood opposite each other in the hall, one below Herbert Olivier's portrait of Herbert Young, the other close to a semi-circular niche with glass doors, which contained Freya's archaeological trophies from Eastern Mediterranean sites.

She led the way upstairs. She indicated a nude sculpture of a stooping girl, on a ledge. 'When the carpenters were here, restoring the tower, they never passed up or down this stair without giving her a little pat, like this!' She chuckled, and caressed the bronze Amazon's posterior. The stair walls were decorated with antique Turkish hand-towels, embroidered with silver and gold thread, framed under glass. The lights had been designed and made as torches. The bedroom was painted the same dusky orange as the hall and its ceiling, like the hall ceiling, comprised the boards and supporting joists of the floor above. All the tower woodwork was stained dark, which showed off the Oriental furnishings and ornaments in an atmosphere of twilight. Bookshelves above the bed contained works by Meredith, R.L. Stevenson and Buchan. There were cartoon sketchbooks by Freya's old friend, Sir Osbert Lancaster; and an entire shelf was devoted to French classics, volumes bound in navy-blue with yellow labels. A ragged little edition of Conrad, I discovered later, contained a story entitled 'Freya of the Seven Isles', and called to mind the Starks' Norwegian ancestry which could be traced as far back as the early eighteenth century. A pair of Turkish bathroom slippers with high blocked soles decorated with mother-of-pearl inlay, lay on a chest of drawers below a heavy mirror, which hung outwards from the wall at a disconcerting, but undoubtedly practical, angle. The wardrobe doors had been made in voluptuous Islamic arches and painted peony-red and gold.

The trapdoor leading to the sitting-room above had been left open. As we emerged into bright daylight, Freya took a deliberate pace or two forward into the room, then turned and said: 'I do beg you, my dear, be careful to close the trapdoor behind you, *always*, when you come up here. A year or two ago, some friends arrived – both getting on in years, like myself. Anyhow, climbed up here and were just about to sit down and relax when the husband saw a little black scorpion crawling on the wall. There . . . just behind where you're standing. He tried to knock it down with a stick but lost his balance and fell through the hatch! Lucky only to have broken an arm and fractured his collar-bone. . . . Might easily have broken his neck!'

I looked around the sitting-room, at the brass Arabian coffee-pots and blue-enamel Persian bowls along the pelmets; the bookcases, packed until their shelves had begun to sag; the table-lamps in pottery and gold-leaf; the Islamic inscriptions; rugs from Bokhara and Samarkand; and sculpture by Freya's father.

An oval table made of beech occupied the centre of the room; the massive boards were nearly two inches thick and the frame was constructed to give four niches, which Freya had designed to hold large illustrated books. The table had been made for Montoria – her previous house not far from Asolo – by the old carpenter, Cadonă, whose shop was a few doors from her apartment in the Via Canova. Cadonă had fashioned all the joinery in the tower and had also built Freya's circular walnut writing-desk, which revolved in a brass guide-rail so that, as she sat working at it, no part of the surface should be inaccessible.

The great polished table beside us had an inscription

inlaid in marquetry in its base. It was a quotation from Freya's favourite Latin poet, Virgil: she repeated the lines from memory: '*Felix qui potuit rerum/Cognoscere causas/Atque metus omnes et inexorabile/Fatum/Subiecit pedibus strepitumque/Acherontis avare.*' She paused, then repeated the final phrase, '*Acherontis avare*', sonorously and with great emotion. 'Wonderful words, aren't they?' she said. 'Thinking of Virgil once when I was ill, I feel certain helped save my life. I've always had a fairly good memory for poetry, which is odd, since my memory for everything else is so erratic. There was another time when I had to lie in bed in a darkened room . . . ill again I suppose! . . . And of course I wasn't able to read, had nobody to talk to and so on. I remembered about five thousand lines of poetry . . . but, you know, it's amazing how it all comes back to you when there are no other distractions of any kind and you're lying quietly alone. It made me realise what I've always known since; that all the information is there in one's wretched brain . . . the secret lies in knowing how to get at it . . . or, rather, what is the key that releases it into the conscious part of the machine.'

All at once she exclaimed: 'However, this won't do! Plenty of time for talk this evening when you come down to supper at the flat. I'm off now to have a little rest . . . perhaps read for a while. That'll leave you free to unpack or do whatever you feel like doing.' She rejected adamantly a suggestion that I might walk with her as far as the Via Canova, assuring me that she was perfectly well able to manage and would, as she put it, 'just totter down slowly', taking her time. I went with her as far as the patio, nevertheless, and watched until she had disappeared from sight among the trees.

During the weeks that followed, we worked together almost every day, choosing photographs from her vast Middle-East collection for a new book, entitled *Rivers of Time*. It was a pleasant occupation which Freya combined with the more arduous revision of transcripts for volumes VII and VIII of her *Letters*. Her energy was remarkable; quite often we worked for twelve hours at a stretch – on one occasion, for fourteen. She appeared virtually unaffected by these marathons.

As time went by, however, and the selections neared completion, we found ourselves once again able to relax and devote a few hours to conversation at the tower.

1

Early Years

THE WIDE windows of the tower sitting-room gave magnificent views of the mountains and their misty foothills. Villas and smallholdings crowded cypress-covered hills that rose in the middle-distance. I turned to Freya, who sat opposite in her faithful green woollen dress, silk cap and pearls, and remarked that this was always how I thought of Italy:

'Hills, sweeping valleys, cypresses and Roman villas. It's beautiful, familiar, yet still it feels quite foreign.'

She replied: 'Well, it can't help seeming foreign . . . after all, you don't live here and you don't speak Italian. So you're bound to find everything a little strange. I've lived in Asolo, off an on, all my life – nearly ninety years – so I must be getting used to it by now!'

'And yet,' I said, 'your mother and father were English and you spent so much of your childhood and adolescence in England. You're English in outlook. How much do you feel part of all this?'

'A part of Asolo . . .?' She nodded thoughtfully. 'Our upbringing was in many ways very unconventional. As you know, my parents were both artists. They enjoyed travelling about and when Vera, my younger sister, and I were little, we used to be carried in wicker baskets tied to donkeys, over the Dolomites on the way to England. You're quite right, I did spend a good deal of my childhood in England, but I also lived for long spells here at Asolo and in Piedmont.'

'So, from the very beginning, Italy was a second home. . . .'

'I would find it hard to say which way round it was, whether England or Italy was home. But I suppose England . . . oh, yes. I think a lot about our lovely house on the edge of Dartmoor, which my father built. It was quite close to Chagford . . . Ford Park was its name. We had a wonderful time there, as children. Father taught Vera and me how to ride and showed us how to fall off, so as not to hurt ourselves. We'd gallop along amongst the heather and throw ourselves headfirst into it, rolling over and keeping ourselves relaxed. I often trip on a carpet or something now, being rather shaky on my feet, but I've remembered always how to fall and so I never do much damage!'

'Did you miss Dartmoor when your parents brought you here to Asolo each year?'

'Oh, yes, missed it dreadfully. There was always plenty to do, however, and I wasn't miserable. Besides, the journey took a long time and helped one to acclimatise. The two ways of life were different and we got different things out of them. We saw Italy and England as really separate worlds. Italy was warm and sunny. We had picnics or went off exploring in the Alps. My cousins used to come and stay with us and we'd walk or ride about on little ponies. . . .'

She sighed. 'But I loved Dartmoor best. Loved the great moorland and the wind and the wild days . . . even the rain and storms.'

'It must have been quite bleak and lonely, though, when you couldn't go out. When the weather was simply too bad.'

'There again, you see, I didn't mind. We had lots of books to read and Vera and I would play chess and other games. Mother and Father got on with their painting or sculpture, or Mother played the piano. Poor Mother hated Dartmoor! Father came back one afternoon in pouring rain, to find her shut up in the drawing-room, with all the curtains drawn and the lamps lit, pretending it was night!'

'Your father was fond of Dartmoor, wasn't he?'

'He absolutely adored it! I suppose, looking back, each of

our parents seemed to go with one or other of these backgrounds. I mean, Mother, who was Papa's first cousin – her own name had also been Stark – had been brought up in Florence. She was used to the sun and the Italian style of living. England didn't appeal to her in the least. Weather, food, everything she found disagreeable. I think poor Father must have had a difficult time with her.'

'Your father seems to have been more adaptable. It was he who discovered Asolo, so to speak. He clearly enjoyed working here – to judge from his pictures – and loved Paris, come to that, where you were born.'

'That's perfectly true. He and Mother should have stayed in Paris, instead of England. They both liked it very much and the big studio in the Rue Denfert Rochereau was pleasant. I went along and had a look at it the other day. Interesting, to discover just where one first set foot upon the earth. I think one always has a special feeling for such places, don't you?'

I then asked Freya why she thought her parents had decided to leave Paris and live a divided life which, despite its romance, in the end had been unsatisfactory.

'I haven't the faintest idea,' she replied, shaking her head. 'I agree entirely. In Paris, they were happy. Father got on with his painting and sculpture, and Mother painted and entertained her friends. Suited them both. And yet, it couldn't have quite, or else why abandon it?'

'Perhaps the attraction of the outdoor life and the Devonshire moors was too strong for your father to resist and likewise Italy for your mother.'

'Something like that must have happened. You see, my dear father had a quiet nature. He liked going off alone with his gun, or riding about. He didn't talk a great deal, but there was always a lot turning over in his mind. Words simply weren't his way of getting thoughts across. He did that through his work as an artist, or by growing fruit and flowers in the garden at Ford Park. He ran much deeper than my mother ever realised: of that I'm quite certain.

'You would have liked my father. He was gentle and strong. Had wonderful hands and such a kind expression. Mother's portrait of him down at the flat is excellent. She got it absolutely right.'

'The other day we were talking about languages. You and your sister, as children, must have had to learn several, just to cope with your various relatives and the nomadic life between Italy and England.'

'By the time Vera and I were four or five, we could speak, apart from English, German and Italian. French we began to learn later, when I was about nine, Vera not quite eight, from our new governess.'

'Who spoke what – assuming it wasn't a complete free-for-all round the dinner-table?'

She laughed. 'You might well think so! But no, each of the languages had its own compartment. Father spoke English, and so we spoke English always to him. Italian was for my mother and German for Granny – I mean, my mother's mother. We didn't get much grasp of the various grammars, of course. It was a question of having conversations rather than writing things down. So, to this day, I don't think I could work out the grammar of a sentence in Italian or German, any more than you would probably be able to deal with the grammar of an English sentence. I mean, one gets it right, or more or less right, but you don't think of the spoken language objectively or analytically.'

On a table beside me lay a big scrapbook containing photographs of Freya at all the various stages of her life up to the age of seventy, and pages of careful notes about her early development, compiled by her mother. I opened the book at random and found the following comment: 'Recites in both languages well. Has an exceedingly good memory . . . absolutely no ear for music.'

Freya grinned broadly as I read out the last line. 'Well, frankly, my dear mother gave me very little encouragement! She herself played the piano beautifully and had been in great demand to play in people's houses, that sort of thing. When she was eighteen, she used to visit the Alma Tadema's in London and talk about painting. The portrait in my hall by Edwin Bale was painted with Mama sitting at Alma Tameda's famous piano, the one with all the famous composers' signatures scratched on the lid. . . . Anyhow, one day I went to her and announced that I, too, would like to play and she replied that there was no reason why not, but that I must be ready to practise for five or six hours every day as she herself had done. Well, that was out of the question, so far as I was concerned! I had other things to do besides; and I had wanted only to play for my own pleasure – not make a career of music. When I told my mother she immediately lost interest and so I never learned to play. I think she would have been terribly severe as a teacher, however, so I didn't regret it all that much!'

'I'm surprised that you could pick up languages so quickly and yet have no ear for music. I've always imagined that the two went together.'

'It does seem strange, but we couldn't help learning other languages when we were small. You see, they were being constantly spoken or read to us, so learning the words and making sentences was automatic. Just like eating or going to sleep. Music was another matter. Mama practised in the drawing-room with the door closed and, if we crept in to listen, she would tell us after a little while to go and see cook in the kitchen or go and play and close the door very quietly behind us. We had to be quiet always when we were little, so that mother could practise the piano in peace.'

'Did you wander off then to see what your father was doing?'

'We adored Father's studio with all the wonderful figures of horses and other animals in it. He'd allow us to watch for a few minutes and then lead us out to the garden. Always being shooed away or asked to leave, it seems!'

I turned the leaves of Freya's *Life History*, pausing at a

page entitled 'Some of Freya Madeline Stark's sayings'. It struck me as a curiously sombre phrase with which to describe the innocent prattle of a tiny child. 'Your sense of humour evidently tickled your mother.'

Freya laid the scrapbook open on her knees and put on her glasses. She bent over it, chuckling. 'Ah yes, this is Mother's handwriting, what does she say? . . . "One day when I was singing a lullaby in which the words 'lean on Mother's warm breast' occurred – Freya asked, 'Mama, what is warm breast?' So I explained it was upon Mother's chest where she was warm & soft. After a meditative silence, Freya said, 'Then my warm breast is here,' placing her hand on the cushions Nature has given her to sit on." ' She laughed loudly as she looked up at me. 'Do you suppose that I really said all that?'

'Well, there it is in writing, if not in print. So it must be true! I like the anecdote your mother has written farther down the page, about her explaining how one's stomach is above and not below one's waist and you seeing her in a low-cut gown and saying, "When I am big I shall dress like Mamma. Mamma does not dress her stomach in the evening." I think that's a marvellous story.'

'Shows how one was understanding and yet not understanding the life about one. It all seems so far away. Awful that we lose that sense of innocence and wonder.'

'Do you honestly believe we do though? Really lose it altogether?'

'Lose is perhaps not the right word. But I don't think we ever get *inside* the feeling of childhood again. Perhaps it's what the man who wrote *Genesis* was saying. When you've tasted the fruit of awareness, the world can never be the same place. Growing up does that to children. We look back at our childhood days, but we can never really look again into that world.'

'And yet Virginia Woolf wrote that the whole charm of Lewis Carroll lay in his ability to do precisely that: to penetrate the crystal that guarded the innocent realm of the child.'

'I see what she means,' Freya replied. 'Difficult to know what makes a work of art successful. Obviously Lewis Carroll, or whatever his real name was, got it right to a large extent, in that children responded to the story. Perhaps the way he treated scale and time and his characters is the secret. The animal characters were very good.'

'As a child, I remember vividly being able to stand beside a bed of lupins and watch bumble-bees, with the lupins and the bees at eye-level. That's how I remember being a boy in summertime – being the same height as the lupins.'

Freya grinned. 'I like that idea very much. It's true, the natural world of animals and flowers means something quite different to us when we're children. I recall something of what I felt about our dogs and the ponies when I was little. They seemed to me very like people, except that they didn't talk and had a rather different arrangement of legs and arms. I had a lovely little Dartmoor pony . . . very affectionate . . . loyal. When I would dismount and unwrap my little packet of bread and whatever cook had given me for lunch, the pony would come up behind me and put its head over, with its nose just here' – she touched her neck where it joined the shoulder – 'eager to have its proper share of the food.

'That's a very clear memory. Me standing there with the pony beside me . . . the sun and the wind and the great spaces of the moor. Wonderful fresh smells of gorse and heather. . . .' Freya sighed again. 'Happy days.'

After a pause, she continued. 'I rode sidesaddle when I was small. Breeches and going astride, like a man, would have been quite unheard of . . . most unbecoming! I wore a warm cloak and had my hair tied back with a bandanna. The little pony knew just where to put his feet and what were safe paths and what were not. One day, however, we went astray and got ourselves into a bog. Father was out riding with me. I came off and landed in the bog . . . the pony got out one side and I floundered out on the other. Father trotted up to find me sitting there wiping myself clean. Gave me rather a ticking-off! Said to me, "You thought first of yourself and not of your horse!" Quite severe, I thought, for somebody who'd just been half-drowned in a bog!'

'Did you resent your father's attitude? Clearly the incident made an impression on you and I'm just wondering what the consequences were, if any?'

'Oh, no, I didn't resent what Father said. At the time, no doubt, I thought, that's a little hard. After all, sitting there covered from head to toe in mud and feeling sorry for myself. Quite natural to feel hard done by, wouldn't you say? I do recollect, though, how Vera and I used to shudder at the thought of keeping our ponies clean and well-brushed and polishing harness. There seemed to be rather too much hard work attached to keeping horses. Father insisted that we do our share, so, I suppose, all the lovely days on Dartmoor had the same tiresome ending – at least we thought it tiresome – of all that brushing down and tidying away in the stables. In fact, I see now how much good that training did one.'

'It must have been magnificent,' I said, 'being free to go for miles over the moor, without fences or gates or restrictions of any kind. It's easy to see how that sort of freedom would influence you in later years, in the sort of life you'd want to lead. I know that, looking back, it's relatively simple to find patterns in one's life – and other people's lives – but I do think that your mountain travels, as a baby, and the Dartmoor life and the mountain life, as a girl, must have steered your thoughts towards travel rather than, say, some sedentary occupation.'

'It is tempting, I agree, to make these links between events or stages of one's life. Sometimes you get it right, but the consequences we see – the results, if you like – generally come from mixed and often very complex origins. I don't think you can say, "Oh, but she loved mountains and riding on the moors, therefore it is quite natural that as a woman she felt drawn to travel and exploration". In my own life, there is probably that connection among a host of others, but then hundreds, if not thousands, of girls ride ponies and go on mountain holidays with their families without plunging into the world of exploration in later life.'

'But surely you wouldn't deny that the freedom you experienced as a child was an important influence?'

'No, of course I wouldn't. As a matter of fact, there's no such thing as total freedom. Take the moors, for example: you shade your eyes and gaze for miles and miles over what seems like endless heather and rock. You might think, "doesn't matter where I go, I'll find the same". But that's just not true. There are dangerous bogs, and hidden sharp stones – hazards of all sorts to beware of. So, you discover, when you take a closer look, that this apparently free country is in reality a web of safe routes where you may go, provided you take care. And life is much the same: there are places where you may go and others where you may not.'

'All this is very interesting, since it appears to emphasise the very Englishness I was talking about earlier. Your father's training, care of animals, weighing up the pros and cons of whatever activity you've planned on. These considered attitudes have an English rather than a Latin quality.'

'Here, again, you must be careful not to make distinctions that are too black and white. Life simply doesn't work this way, as I keep on saying. . . . I think that you're right, nevertheless, that animals have a better time in England, whereas, in Italy, children have a wonderful life. Nothing is too much trouble for the parents, every wish, every whim, is catered for. Italian children have a happy time of it!'

She went on: 'Thinking about what you were saying a moment ago, about the moorland without fences or gates, reminded me of something that happened after I'd grown up. I was staying with a friend in Wales – might have been Venetia Buddicom – and I was riding home after a day out. As I went through a gate, the metal tore my foot, right through the bootleather; made a terrible wound. You know, I didn't look down at it, for I knew I would have fainted; but instead I dismounted and closed the open gate before we went on. Then I told my friend what had happened. Imagine doing that anywhere except in England! Shows what one's early training meant: never leave a gate standing open after you've gone through. That was my dear father, once again.'

'What else did you do as children?'

'Oh, played with our dolls, and went swimming and read a good deal. Vera was more outdoors inclined even than I was. I'd be quite content to sit and read a book, exactly as I do now. I didn't have to be amused all the time, and in fact rather enjoyed my own company – that is, mine and Vera's. We used to feel quite cross when other children arrived and we had to play with them when we'd much rather have been off doing our own things. Our parents used to get quite desperate, but it was simply that we didn't need other children's company and in fact didn't want it.'

'From what you say, it sounds almost as if you were aggressive as a child. Though I find it difficult to believe.'

'I remember one time when some boys came to stay – relations of some sort – and one of them, quite a big boy, complained to my mother that I bullied him. I mean it was absurd. He was about twice my age and enormous by comparison. Anyhow, Mother asked me to treat him more gently, and that was that.'

'And did you?'

She chuckled. 'No, of course not! Carried on exactly as before.'

'Your mother dressed you and Vera quite romantically, even for the end of last century. Look at some of these pictures in the scrapbook: striped smocks and big straw hats. . . . And look at this snapshot where you're wearing lacing-boots and breeches. That must have been unusual. . . . You seem to have dressed up a lot. . . . Look here, a sort of Grecian robe with sandals and a crown of leaves. Did you enjoy dressing up like that?'

'Yes . . . yes, I think so. After all, it's something that all little girls want to do. Sometimes in Italy when the weather was hot, we played in the garden without any clothes on at all. Herbert Young took some photographs of us. Quite a lot of these he took . . . the ones with the Japanese parasols and that one of us up a tree. Do you see how long my hair was, even then? By the time I was twelve, it hung down below my waist. Lovely long brown hair to my waist. . . .' Freya sat quietly for a few moments, deep in recollection. I wondered whether to ask her about the grisly accident which occurred when she was thirteen, when she was half-scalped by an electric loom at the silk-factory which her mother looked after in Piedmont. When she began to speak again, however, it was on a different subject.

'I can't quite make it out, what my mother wrote here . . . something to do with words.'

I took the open book from her and examined the entry, written in her mother's strong, sloping hand. 'I think it says – "Has a good sense of rythm [*sic*] and rhyme & of the exact meaning of words." Then it goes on – "Is extremely observant, displays a good deal of tact & great wish to please – Also much self-control. . . . Her desire for approval might interfere with her straightforwardness in time. At present she is quite truthful." What do you make of that?'

'Well, I don't think I've ever been deliberately untruthful, although I daresay, for reasons of tact, as my dear mother observed, one has to modify things. There's no point in hurting somebody needlessly, just in order to speak the truth. You have to exercise some discretion. Some aspects can be mentioned, others avoided. But that's only civilised behaviour . . . not sheer deviousness. Interesting what she writes about the meaning of words . . . that's correct I think. I've always been at some pains to get straight what I want to say. Of course, it's meant that, in later life, as a writer, I've tended to work very slowly . . . steadily and regularly, but very, *very*, slowly. Where that comes from, I don't honestly know . . . whether from Father's or Mother's side; or perhaps from much farther back, from some ancestor who lived centuries ago, whom I've never heard of. That's such a fascinating idea, isn't it? That we are all made of the stuff of all these years going back heaven knows how far!'

'What about being straightforward? Do you think your mother might have had a point there? Although the other day, somebody told me that you like nothing better than a good argument, with plenty of differences of opinion that you can get your teeth into. That doesn't seem to fit the placid childhood character and desire for approval at any cost.'

Freya sat forward and eyed me intently. 'Let's be quite clear about this! I quite definitely don't like argument for argument's sake. That's just boring. There's really nothing worse than having to explain and qualify every word you utter or find yourself in company with somebody who shares nothing of your beliefs. Terribly hard work that and frankly disagreeable. I think I was fairly good-tempered as a child, fairly happy and contented always. Vera was a sweet little thing, you know, and a wonderful companion. She was sixteen months younger, much more outgoing and, I think, much prettier than me. However, we didn't have rows and I don't remember having to be disciplined very often. Just once or twice perhaps for some small thing I'd done. Certainly I wouldn't now bend over backwards to avoid an argument about a subject I felt strongly about, but I would rather have a discussion without too many fundamental differences, which might lead to a more constructive result.'

'Surely a companion who agrees with you all the time must grow a little tedious? Some gentle disagreement of the purely intellectual sort adds salt to the meat.'

'Ah, yes, just so long as it isn't overdone! I'm not for a moment suggesting that my hypothetical companion – he or she – should reply with a simple "yes" to everything one utters. That would be quite hopeless, of course. But the grind of continual justification and explanation of one's basic philosophies tends to be an end in itself. You go home, having bared your innermost soul, but having left the original subject – politics, art, literature, or whatever – quite untouched. . . . I'm not putting this very well, but I mean it's so pleasant when one can dispense with all that – get right to the heart of the discussion and leave the personality out of it.'

'Were you encouraged to talk a great deal as a child?'

She shook her head. 'No, not really. Father didn't talk much himself and Mother was always sitting alone with a book, or playing Chopin or Liszt or painting. One governess chatted to us in French and, in Italy, dear old Herbert Young, our next-door-neighbour here in Asolo, used to read stories from the Classics to Vera and me. I imagine he must have talked to us quite a lot, but I can't remember now what about!'

'This gives an absolutely conventional picture of the late-Victorian household. Parents going about their own business; children, well looked-after but seen rather than heard.'

'You mustn't forget about my parents being artists. Artists need a good deal of peace to do their work. Children running everywhere and making a noise would be a dreadful distraction. Mind you, I like children of all ages very much, the tiny ones especially. We had a wonderful governess, Coccola – dear, darling Coco! – and we used to ride our bicycles and go about with her.'

'You were telling me just now how dangerous the moor could be. I presume when you and your sister were very small, five or six let's say, your father or some other older person must have gone with you. Someone like Coco.'

'Yes, of course. Dear Coco appeared when I was about nine and we'd all bicycle about the countryside round here, have picnics at Belluno and so forth. . . . Father was my chief companion on Dartmoor. Vera and I used to walk with him hand in hand, one on either side. Mother made a little painting of us. We were both wearing awful, long black stockings over our knees.'

'There must have come a time when you were able to wander off by yourself without someone to look after you.'

Freya grinned. 'Well, you know, I started wandering off when I was very young – caused quite a lot of excitement at home, I may say! Once, at Yelfords, when I was four, Mr Reid, our postman, found me setting out for Plymouth to be a cabin-boy. Four is a bit young isn't it, even for a cabin-boy! I must have heard about the life from one of Father's stories. *Treasure Island* or some such adventure. Certainly I was too small to have read about it myself.'

'What happened next?' I asked.

'The postman was very nice . . . asked where I was going and what I was going to do. I told him. Then he asked if I had any money. I said, yes, I had one shilling and sixpence. He replied that that wasn't nearly enough and I had better go home and get some more. Then he took my hand and led me back to the house. The whole family was out looking for me by this time, but Mother and Father weren't cross, just relieved that I was all right.'

'I don't believe for a moment that that put an end to your early wanderings. From what you say, the wanderlust was already too deeply ingrained.'

'Indeed, it was! There was another time, I remember, a year or two later. We had another house, at Farnham, in Surrey, close to the common. Somebody in the family, might have been an aunt or possibly it was Father, had given me a book of fairy-tales containing a story about a sea-witch. I made up my mind immediately to go in search of the sea-witch, who, I was sure, lived on the far side of the common. When they eventually found me, I was already several miles away, tottering slowly along!'

'What sort of reception did you get this time, when you were brought home?'

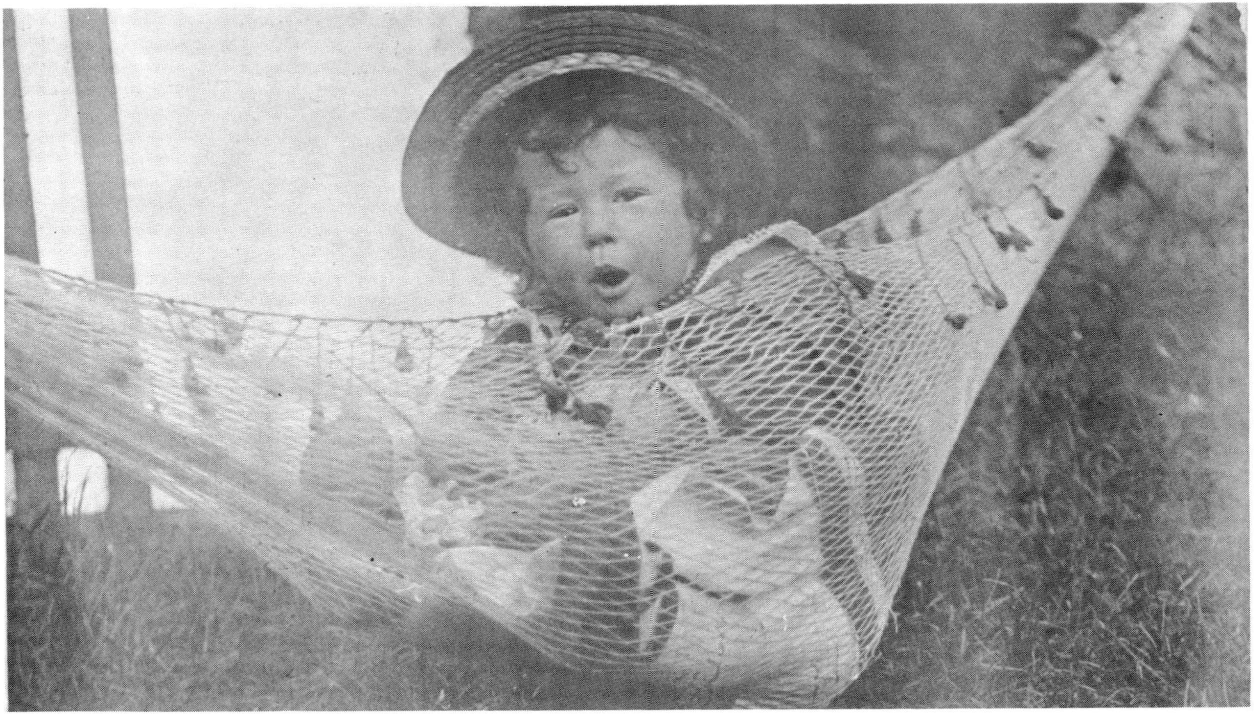

Freya Stark at the age of one (*photograph by Herbert Young*)

Freya riding at Ford Park, Dartmoor, *c.* 1900

Freya at home in Asolo, 1902 (*photograph by Herbert Young*)

In summer regalia at Asolo, 1902 (*photograph by Herbert Young*)

Freya and Vera playing in their garden at Asolo, 1905 (*photograph by Herbert Young*)

'Although my parents were very pleased to see me, I received some gentle criticism . . . was told that in future I should say first of all where I was going, what I meant to do, and so on. I remember thinking it very strange that everyone should be so anxious, and strangest of all that I should have been reprimanded.'

I asked Freya whether she regretted the passing of her childhood days, which, on the whole, seemed to have been happy and secure and had provided her in later years with pleasant memories.

'How fortunate you were, too,' I added, 'to experience a way of life which came to a sudden end with the First World War. You must have felt very sad to see it disappear.'

'My feelings about those far-away days are rather mixed, you know. Sometimes when I sit here, or down in the flat, and think over all we did, I feel sad that it's gone, not just from me – beyond my grasp – but from the world. At other times, I feel that I don't really care. After all, every age has its own peculiar attractions, just as it has drawbacks. It's quite wrong to wish that Time would stand still.'

'Are you aware of any striking differences between the world you knew as a little girl and the world we live in today? I mean quite small personal details rather than immense political issues.'

'Quite so. Anyhow, as a child the big political movements don't really affect one. Certainly there are differences. For instance, our whole environment in 1900 was infinitely quieter: just imagine – no wireless, no aeroplanes, no cars or buses, at least hardly any; no machine to play records, no television. Life went along much more slowly and I think moved pretty much at walking pace, or the speed at which a horse could draw a carriage or cart. Galloping your pony was real speed! You never went faster than that, anywhere – unless by train.

'People often remark that the whole place seemed cleaner in those days. I wonder if that's really true?'

'Well, I suppose it must be, in the sense that there were no engines and far fewer chemicals about. On the other hand, hygiene has improved immeasurably in our own day and other aspects of health, such as medicine and sanitation generally. However, the countryside was quite wonderful – a real paradise for children. Of course, the summers were invariably sunny. Silly to think so, but you know, looking back, it does seem to me that they were. I think poor people had a bad time of it, though. There was a lot of hardship in England – perhaps not so much where we were, in the country. But the cities must have been pretty dreadful places.'

'Asolo must have been tremendously different, too, seventy or eighty years ago.'

'Yes and no. Again, the changes have come about with such things as motor-cars and buses and the wireless. Transport and communications, we might say, have altered life as much as anything. I mean, apart from the shops that have sprung up all over the town, in basements, and the cars crowding into the Piazza at weekends, there's not much altered from my earliest recollections. Oh, telephone and electricity wires and the wires sticking up on the house-roofs. . . .'

'Television aerials. . . ?'

'I think that's what they're for. Make a terrible mess of the landscape. . . . Yes, that's where the obvious changes are. But then there's a whole variety of change of a more subtle kind – people's dress, manners, speech and general habits. I think that in my youth there was a feeling of contentment that's gone as the consequence of two world wars. People are restless nowadays . . . need to be entertained and excited all the time. Whether that's good or bad, I don't know, but I don't really care for the atmosphere it creates . . . a kind of tension everywhere.'

'You sound glad that you were born when you were, in the 1890s, unless you wish you'd been born fifty years earlier. I presume not fifty years later!'

Freya shook her head and tapped the arm of her chair, as she considered the question. 'Being born, like dying, is mercifully something quite beyond our control – well looked after, I feel sure, by the Almighty – they're really the same thing, doors to another world, one of which we come in by to this life and one by which we leave. But since there is no way in which I or anyone can influence the timing of these appearances and disappearances in terms of the point of history at which they occur, it would be foolish to regret one's birthday – indeed to feel apprehensive about the day one dies.'

'Were your parents very religious?' I asked. 'You don't often speak about religion in terms of this or that faith; and especially not where you yourself are concerned.'

'My mother of course was Church of England. Father had been brought up as a Presbyterian, I think. But, whatever they felt about religion themselves, when we were small, they left it completely open, which I'm by no means sure was a good thing. Neither Vera nor I were baptised as babies – in my case, not until I was about nineteen. I feel now that it would have helped to have something to hold on to, as a guide, when we were little. Not just be cast adrift, so to speak. But that's what happened, and we didn't know anything different.'

'I remember an essay, I think it's in *Perseus in the Wind*, where you describe your feelings at an early age, when you were told that your mother wouldn't live for a thousand years: in other words, that neither she nor you were immortal. You cried and felt terribly unhappy. Might some inkling of God have helped you to feel better?'

'I doubt it. I was much too young to understand. But the sense of impermanence that flooded through to me when Nurse told me was a dreadful experience. I still remember it and how it happened: standing up in bed in my flannelette nightdress, ready to go to sleep. I wept and wept: couldn't bear it! Now of course, I feel quite opposite thoughts about death and the whole question of mortality. I would be horrified to be told that I'd go on living for ever, unless perhaps this age business could be solved by other means. As a child you're full of energy and able to tackle anything that comes your way. There are no terrible hurts that last and the whole world's fresh and waiting to be discovered. These spring days of one's life were wonderful. Now I'm happy and ready to go at any time . . . well, it would be nice to do just one or two more journeys before bidding life farewell . . . perhaps see the Himalayas again. That's the trouble, you know, one would need two or three lives to do it all!'

'I would like to hear more about the people with whom you came into contact most, as a child. Let's see . . . there'd be your mother and father; Vera of course; various nurses and cousins, grandparents – all these.'

'Oh, yes, and don't forget dear Herbert Young here at Asolo. Always very kind to us as children. There were people, like Granny, whom I remember vividly as striking or unusual or in some way interesting; but as far as people whose presence had a lasting effect upon my life, I would say that parents and sister and dear old Herbert were the main ones when I was small.'

2

Spheres of Early Influence

'YOU REFER continually to your parents as artists and seem always at pains to separate the needs of artists from the needs of other people.'

'Well that's because their needs to a large extent *are* different! Look, an artist, whether he or she happens to be a painter or a writer or a musician, doesn't matter what form the art takes, must have peace and concentration in order to work. Distractions break the flow of ideas and very often that's hard to get back. I'm not trying to put artists on a pedestal, or ascribe any very peculiar qualities to them; all I'm saying is that their work, which uses a lot of nervous energy and tends to be lonely, depends on absence of distractions.

'Of course, my mother had an idea of business as well as being an artist. . . . After all, she ran our silk-factory for many years, kept that going. There was order in her life and a strong sense of discipline.'

'I'd associated discipline more with your father. But maybe that followed from my idea of the Victorian family.'

'Actually, neither Father nor Mother were strict enough with themselves where work was concerned. They worked hard enough, when they worked; make no mistake about it. But they allowed too many other interests to interfere. Mother would go off arranging a big lunch-party for their friends, or Papa would get absorbed with planting shrubs and flowers in the garden. Or he might go out hunting with the local pack, or go shooting with our neighbours. In these respects my parents were much too easily distracted from their real work as artists.'

'Might it have made a difference if they hadn't been fairly well-off and had to work for a living?'

'No question about it! Of course it would. . . . However, there's no guarantee either, that hardship or poverty would have made them better painters.'

'Did your parents think of themselves as successful painters or didn't they bother with such things?'

'To be honest, I don't know how they regarded their own work. I suppose, like everybody else, they felt pleased when a picture or a little bronze turned out right; and equally depressed when it didn't. But that's quite usual. . . . Artists – I'll be more exact, writers – cannot judge very accurately when a book is good, or when it has specially fine things in it. One doesn't have that view of one's own work; and frankly I don't believe writers who maintain that they do.'

'Your mother and father were what we would term, nowadays, amateur artists. Is that fair comment?'

'If you insist on finding a category for them – yes, that's all right. But, now look, what does all this mean – this business of amateur and professional? Most people separate the two by involving money. If you work for payment, you're a professional; if you don't you're amateur. There is another distinction implied, however, which suggests that the amateur is somehow less efficient. Probably because he doesn't devote himself to whatever the work is full-time, and does it for pleasure rather than as a living. Personally, I quite fail to understand why one can't do both: make a living from one's art or whatever it is, and derive pleasure from it at the same time.'

'The term amateur is more closely associated with the nineteenth century than with the present day, though. I mean, there were amateur scientists, biologists, sportsmen . . . all men and women of independent means and making a huge contribution to knowledge. But surely that day is over?

Science and sport are evolving too quickly and the standards demanded have raised an insuperable barrier between the amateur and the professional.'

'Well, I can't answer for such matters as sport and science. However, might one say this? In sport, you're dealing with a single objective at a time: jumping over a stick, or throwing a javelin further than another competitor. I quite see that, within reason, the more you practise doing whatever sport it is, the better you get. Excellence in this instance seems to me to derive from repetition, rather like a juggler practising with his clubs. The more he does it, the more expert he becomes.

'The artist's task is not like that. A writer who has nothing to say will never produce anything *of substance*, even if he were to work for twenty-four hours a day, every day of his life. The actual writing might improve, in fact, almost certainly would do so; but there would be nothing much else – no real life that breathes, nothing worth writing about.'

'But to go back to your parents. Do you think their work remained static? You've more or less said that they would have painted better if they'd worked more consistently.'

'That's right. I think they had each something to say in their art. A more regular routine of work might have brought that out more clearly. They were essentially realist painters. Somebody who knew what he was talking about once told me that my mother's portrait of Granny reminded him of a Monet. Father painted beautiful little landscapes all round Asolo and some really wonderful pictures of Dartmoor. But Father will be remembered best for sculpture; animal studies, like the rhinoceros in the Tate.'

'I take it that the artistic hub of your parents' lives was here in Asolo, rather than Dartmoor or Farnham?'

Freya considered the point carefully. 'Asolo had attracted artists since Browning's day. They came here and rented houses, exactly as my parents did. There was quite a little colony of painters at one time. Pen Browning, Herbert Young, the Oliviers . . . all good friends of our family.'

'Whereas, in England, your neighbours were most probably gentlemen farmers and landed folk.'

'Yes. I remember Father going off hunting and men coming up and greeting him and saying, "Good morning, Stark." I liked all that very much: the hunting and the solid country atmosphere of the moor. There was an atmosphere of good-neighbourliness which impressed us even as children. You felt part of that landscape.'

'And Asolo?'

'Asolo, too, in another way. I can't express just what the differences were. It's all too long ago, and, as we've been saying, one looks back at childhood with changed vision. Really a matter of looking into one world from another, like an astronomer, through a telescope. . . . You see moving pictures of yourself, but what went on here,' Freya tapped her forehead, 'that remains a mystery.'

'You were clearly very devoted to Herbert Young,' I said.

Her face lit up at the mention of Young's name and she began to speak with enthusiasm:

'Dear old Herbert! He and Papa and Pen Browning came first to Asolo together. Pen Browning already had several villas here; then Papa and Herbert decided they would stay. That was probably a hundred years ago. Dreadful, isn't it. . . ! What a relic one sometimes feels! Herbert was Australian, quite well-off, highly cultivated and passionately fond of Renaissance architecture and painting. Loved photography and was always to be seen with his camera, and the wooden legs it sat upon, under his arm. He painted quite well, but photography was his greater interest, I think. Have you seen his photographs?'

I said that I had and commented on how faded they appeared.

'He always quite deliberately brought too much light into his pictures. Evidently preferred them to look faded. I'm not absolutely sure why Herbert liked this effect – it may have been that he saw photography as a branch of painting and tried to achieve the same results as he did with oils or watercolours.'

'What did Herbert Young look like?'

She screwed up her eyes, concentrating hard. 'He had rather a nice sort of face. Very gentle, like my father's but not so strongly made. I imagine he was getting to be middle-aged when Vera and I were children. He had a big moustache and wore a straw hat, like all the others. And he had very pale blue eyes. The portrait of dear Herbert downstairs in the entrance hall, by Herbert Olivier, is a good likeness, at whatever age he was then.'

'What happened when you went up into the mountains: did he come with you?'

'Oh, yes, quite frequently. We would go off to one of the Alpine valleys, somewhere in Piedmont and then Herbert would come along later, riding his bicycle. He would take about four days to cycle up from Asolo to our little inn . . . never hurried. He'd go along and then find some church, or hear of a fresco somewhere on the way; and so he would detour off to have a look and spend the night either in an hotel or just sleep in the hedgerow, wherever he happened to be. Pleasant way to get about. . . . There is the question of time, of course. Not everybody can linger over a journey as they'd like to, although, no doubt about it, the journey is the main ingredient of serious travel.'

'Going back to photography for a moment . . . it occurs to me that Herbert Young might have encouraged you, however indirectly, to take a camera with you, when you began to travel later on.'

'Who can tell, where these things are concerned? I don't think he ever encouraged me in any definite way. No doubt by then I was used to the idea of photography and seeing records kept of our childhood, parents' friends, little expeditions we'd made . . . that type of thing. So, when I came to travel in Persia and Arabia it was natural to think of bringing a camera, as well as keeping a diary. But to give a straight answer would be difficult; the fact that Herbert was always about the place and taking photographs may have made a deeper impression than one realised.'

'The friendship with Herbert Young spanned a good many years of your life, yet somehow he remains in the shadows. Only now and then steps forward, you might say, to the front of the stage.'

'If you count right through from earliest childhood, I should think Herbert knew me for the better part of fifty years . . . quite a big slice of time. He was very nice and quiet, chivalrous; concerned a good deal for our welfare. I would describe him, other things apart, as having been a thoroughly good, kind man. Then, as you know, he made over his house to me, so that Mother and I would always have a home and security; also take care of his beloved Casa Freia. That was in 1926. But he went on living at the Casa Freia until he died at the beginning of the Second World War. We just came and went as circumstances dictated. Of course, by that time, my father and mother had ceased to live together and Father had gone off to farm in Canada.'

'The break-up of your parents' marriage must have been very upsetting for you, especially as it meant that your father decided to live so far away.'

Freya looked sadly out of the window. 'Yes . . . yes . . . I missed my father dreadfully. But, you know, one could see it coming for years. He and my mother were poles apart as far as mutual interests were concerned and I think only our being children kept them together for these last years. They were quite faithful to each other, however; I am sure of that. Father never looked at another woman and Mama, although she'd lots and lots of admirers, behaved honourably. The only mistake was her friendship with the man who married my sister. My mother did everything she could to encourage Vera to marry him, while I did all I could to prevent her. I knew Vera would be miserable and so she was; but it was only years afterwards, after Vera had died, that my mother admitted what a blunder she'd made.'

'I'm a little puzzled as to why your father decided on Canada, rather than somewhere in Europe. I can see why he should have preferred Canada to the United Sates, since it was a part of the Empire and his whole personality was so English. On the other hand, his training and his art were European and his way of life had been European rather than colonial. I find it particularly strange that he should have cut adrift from Dartmoor, which he loved so much.'

'On the face of it, Father's decision was an odd one, I admit. What happened was that the government of the day introduced a tax on minerals. There were some old workings on our land, which hadn't been mined for heaven knows how many years. Quite useless. . . . Nevertheless, Father was required to pay the taxes and I suppose that was the final straw. He said, "England is no longer a country fit for a gentleman to live in!" He sailed for British Columbia and bought the Broken Hill Ranch at Creston.'

'Perhaps he simply didn't want to live amongst all the things that reminded him of the past – when you were all together.'

'Yes, it might have been that. . . .'

3

Adolescence

WE LEFT the subject of Freya's parents and began to talk about her early education. She maintained that it had been haphazard, to begin with.

'Very strange, you know . . . plenty of books about the house always and a cultured atmosphere. But nobody – neither Mother nor Father – took an active interest in our education as such. And yet, it's not quite true to say that either. Mother read to us, or talked to us before dinner, in our room upstairs. And Father would explain everything about flowers and trees and animals when we went for walks with him. Of course, my sister and I loved those country walks when the whole world came alive round about us. . . . What I'm really getting at is that there were no formal lessons until our governess arrived.'

'Judging from your books, you don't appear to have been starved of learning. You evidently thrived on the hedgerow system!'

'Like some little bird waiting on the rim of the nest to be fed. . . .' She laughed at the image of herself as a fledgling. Then she said: 'But we didn't do too badly. By nine, I spoke four languages and had started to read the English authors – I daresay not understanding it all, but dipping into that world, nevertheless. Father had taught us a lot about Nature and we lived all the time among pictures and music and artistic discussion. Travelling to Italy must have opened our eyes to the rest of life. . . .'

'What about such things as mathematics and geography?'

'As I say, geography we were learning from practical experience and what we didn't gain in this fashion, no doubt Coco, our dear governess, drilled in. As for mathematics, I've never had any aptitude for them. Simple addition and subtraction has always cost me infinite labour, particularly now.'

'Presumably any gaps there were got filled when you went off to complete your education in London. . . . Very curious, however, that neither of your parents tried to encourage you to study art. I'd have imagined they would have been delighted had you shown an interest in painting.'

'Quite the opposite. I received no encouragement whatever. In fact, they made it clear they believed I'd no talent at all for painting and so, that was that.'

'Did that upset you?'

'No, not unduly. I might have thought it a little hard to have it written off quite so bluntly. Anyhow, I had started to write little scraps of poetry, all of it terribly bad; and so already had a foothold in literature. . . .'

'Your parents seem to have been somewhat extremist in the matter of education. Rather a case of all or nothing.'

'It strikes one so, doesn't it?' she said. 'Think of my mother – all interest in me learning to play the piano vanished like smoke when I explained I wanted to play only for pleasure. No question of being encouraged to draw and paint, unless I would do it seriously – such severe standards for amateurs! And yet, they themselves not taking their art quite seriously enough. . . . What a mixture! Long before our governess, I learned to read from posters in the street. I expect Vera did the same.'

'How old were you when you began to write poetry?'

She thought hard. 'About twelve or thirteen. Might have been a little sooner. But I don't think there's anything so very significant about that. I had some creative instinct, that goes without saying, and so had to get whatever feelings there were out of my system. Painting and music were closed doors, it appears, and so I turned to writing. Still, that's hardly exceptional, as I say.'

'As you grew older, doubtless you became increasingly aware that your mother and father were not getting on well together. That must have created a disturbing atmosphere, no matter how tactful they were.'

She nodded. 'Of course. Vera and I both felt sad that they couldn't be happier together. But they behaved unselfishly and gave very little hint of their feelings toward each other. Mother would take my sister and me to Italy, while Papa stayed behind at Ford Park. All our lives, they'd tended to keep to separate ends of the house, each doing his or her own work. But, yes, we did feel it, although it's too strong to describe the atmosphere as having been disturbing.'

'In the *Life History* scrapbook,' I said, 'your mother wrote with evident pride that, by the time you were five, you had begun to show considerable self-control. From what you've just told me, self-control was clearly a family characteristic.'

Again Freya nodded. 'I should say that's true. My parents were both controlled about their emotions, and Vera and I were taught to be brave and, for example, contain fear. I remember Father would give us sixpence if we'd walk through a little wood at dusk and touch the fence at its far side, then walk back. Running wouldn't do – we had to walk. I used to feel some awful thing behind me, feel it right between my shoulders, as though it were following. Anyhow, we were absolutely truthful and went and touched the fence and came back and each received sixpence. Quite a lot for little girls of five or six to do. There's something very English in that, you know. We felt we had to *do* it. . . It was like going to play in the lane outside Ford Park. Mother gave strict instructions that we might play along the grass verge, but forbade us to so much as step on to the lane itself. We obeyed her without question. It might sound incredible now, a little too good to be true; but that was our world, and courage and obedience were important.'

'Do you think this early and quite rigorous training helped you to bear the consequences of the accident that happened when you were thirteen?'

'It might have helped, I suppose. My poor mother felt that life was over for me. But it wasn't, you see. . . .' She looked down at her hands, flexing her fingers. 'I had such long hair when I was thirteen. Wore it loose, right down to my waist. I was standing in the silk-factory in Piedmont – Mario, who became Vera's husband, owned it and my mother ran it for him. There was a new electric loom with a spindle that went nearly to the roof. The draught it made running sucked in my long hair and I was pulled hard against the spindle, my head right up against it and feet flying horizontally, whirling round and round. My feet kept hitting the walls. Mario rushed up and wrenched me free. The loom tore off half my scalp and my right ear and eyelid. Nearly killed me. I remember my mother's face as she saw me being carried away. . . . When the doctor was sewing back my eyelid, I remember asking why was he using a packing-needle? In fact, he was using the finest possible needle, but a packing-needle was what it felt like.'

'I read your description of the accident in your first volume of autobiography, *Traveller's Prelude*, and was impressed by two aspects: first of all, the precision with which you had recalled the feelings and sensations of the actual moment, and also the fact that you'd experienced no pain.'

'Well you see, I didn't lose consciousness while the machine was spinning me round and so was able to take some notice of what was happening. I don't think I felt afraid, but that had no doubt something to do with the shock of being pulled off my feet without warning.' She snapped her fingers. 'Happened just like that! I didn't feel much pain as far as I remember, until the doctors in Turin – where I was taken – began to remove skin grafts from my legs to replace the missing scalp. That was sheer agony; I've never experienced pain like it at any time in my life, either before or since.'

'After you got better, did you feel self-conscious or shy as a result of what had been done to you? It must have been particularly difficult, being a girl.'

'That was what troubled my dear mother. But the surgeons were extremely skilful. There was scarcely any visible damage when the scars healed, and I wore a hairpiece over the rest. Very often a big hat, which in any case was the fashion. I don't wear a wig any longer, but, as you know, I have these little caps of silk or lace, like the one I'm wearing today, which are rather pretty; and, most recently of all, I've taken to wearing a combination of the lace-cap under one of my big hats. But that's come along with age. Works very well, don't you think?'

'Changing course slightly – the imagery of long, flowing hair appears in early poems you wrote about this period – beginning a year or two after the accident, about nineteen-eight.'

'I should think that's quite likely. It was a terrible thing for a little girl to lose most of her hair like that. . . . Whether I wrote about it consciously or unconsciously, I've no idea. Incidentally, do you like those early poems?'

'Yes, I do on the whole. I'm no judge of poetry, but many of your sad poems have a strong lyrical quality.'

'Oh, really? Have they?'

'Yes, I think they do. Others are rather too sentimental for me. Anyhow, I have an impression that you always dismiss your poetry as juvenile and inconsequential.'

'Perhaps I ought to dismiss most of it. The early poems, I mean, written between the ages of about twelve and thirty. I've written poetry off and on since then. . . some things not too bad.

'My dear godfather, W.P., thought most of the early stuff rather poor, though he liked one or two. Can't remember which they were. It's so hard for a writer to judge his or her own work.'

'I'd be amazed if you haven't a very shrewd idea of which

On a road through Andorra, 1923

Freya in Arab dress, Lebanon, 1928

In Baghdad, 1937

Freya, aged thirty-five

poems come off and which don't.'

'Well now . . . where prose is concerned I wouldn't argue. I have been writing constantly for more than fifty years and must have learned something about my trade by now. I still stand by what I was saying to you earlier, however. It's virtually impossible for any writer to know if he's done something good – particularly at the time. Years and years afterwards, he might have a better notion.

'Perhaps one could say that a writer sees the good bits like lights winking far away through a dark night. You can't imagine what they signify, but they give you a hint of something there. . . . Occasionally, your feeling about what you've written is more positive, but I should say that's rare.'

I said: 'You met your godfather, W.P. Ker, a year or two after you'd begun to write poetry – verse . . . call it what you like. The middle 'teens are such formative, highly sensitive years. . . . I can't help wondering if W.P.'s criticisms didn't put you off writing poetry, rather than any disinclination of your own.'

'Dear W.P. left me in no doubt about his views on what I had written; but he always had a regard for my feelings. His criticism was severe sometimes, but never, I would say, harsh. No, I think I realised myself after a time that I wasn't going to be a poet – that prose was more my line. But even that revelation didn't strike me until years after W.P. had died. Nevertheless, I loved language and words and, of course, so did he and we used to talk for hours about that.'

'He was one of the sources of inspiration and a profound influence,' I said. 'He gave your life new direction and drive; just as your parents and Herbert Young had influenced you most in childhood. Who else was there apart from him?'

'What period are you talking about exactly?'

'Oh, roughly from the time you went to school in London until after the First World War. Up until you began travelling in the Middle East.'

She sat back, thinking carefully. 'Well, W.P. was the main

one to start with. He took everything in – literature, mountaineering, history, languages. His friendship was very important and a very great joy besides. . . . There was old Doughty, whom I never met, but whose book, you know – the *Arabia Deserta* – got me off to Baghdad and out among the Arabs . . . then there was Viva Jeyes. I lodged with Viva at her house in Grove End Road while I was studying at Bedford College. It was darling Viva who first introduced me to W.P.'

4

W.P.

'I'D NO idea what W.P. would be like – Viva's description was rather off-putting to say the least! She said, "There's a dried-up old Scottish professor of literature coming tonight. Hope you won't be too bored by him." He was quite elderly, about sixty. I was just a girl. . . .'

'Did his appearance match the description?'

'I expect it did,' Freya answered, smiling. 'He had white hair, thin on top. Wore rimless glasses. Had a kindly expression, I thought. But he didn't talk very much except when he had really got something he wanted to say. . . . The rest of his appearance was fairly ordinary – I mean he wore the sort of dark clothes you'd take for granted. He was, in any case, very conservative.'

I asked Freya what had attracted her to Ker. 'It must have been something less obvious than physical appearance or charm. Besides, a sixty-year-old Scots professor of literature is strong stuff for a teen-age girl.'

'I daresay. But, you know, I felt magnetised by W.P.'s intellect and also by a great spiritual warmth he seemed to possess. It wasn't infatuation, let me add. It was really the immense power of his mind that drew me.'

'Can you remember what you talked about?'

'I remember W.P. talked about books and languages . . . all subjects that greatly interested me. But that first night at Viva's he didn't go on at length.'

'I suppose being a dinner-party and with other guests there conversation got fragmented.'

'Perhaps. Actually it was quite a small party; I can't remember just how many people, or even who the others were, but I should have imagined six or eight of us – no more. Shows how my attention was riveted on W.P.' She paused. 'W.P. and I didn't sit next to each other at dinner; that I do recall. I remember seeing him across the table, more or less opposite. No, we didn't talk together during dinner, at least not a great deal.'

'And yet this evening clearly stands out as a landmark in your early life.'

'Well, after dinner we must have talked more. I think that was it. . . . W.P. mentioned that he'd planned to climb in the Dolomites that August and I invited him to join us at the little inn where we would stay during the summer – mother, Vera, myself and various cousins and friends. He agreed at once and came to Italy pretty well every year after that.'

'From what you say, W.P. doesn't strike one immediately as having been an outdoorsman. I can grasp the academic picture, but I find it hard to imagine him scrambling up and down mountains.'

'In fact, I haven't described W.P. very well. He was thin and strong. Strength was quite evident. You saw both sides of him straight away: the intellectual side and the outdoor side. That intrigued me, as it would, I imagine, most people. He was about average height for a man. He taught me most of what I ever learned about climbing . . . many other things besides.'

She told me how she used to attend Ker's lectures at London University, as an extra-mural student, while she was still at Bedford College. She would walk through Regent's Park to Gower Street and sit in the lecture-hall with Ker's other students. 'That was about 1912. Whenever he came into the hall, the class would greet him by drumming their feet on the floorboards – like this!' Freya stamped her feet on the sitting-room floor. 'Wonderful to see his effect on those rowdy boys!'

'Why do you think he was so successful as a lecturer?'

'Difficult to pin down . . . force of intellect, charisma, ali that would have played a part. . . . However, more important, I think, was his way of confiding in students. Making each one feel involved in an intimate discussion of whatever writer's work it was. Never preached at them or talked down to them. I believe that might have been his secret – part of it anyway.'

In Italy Freya and Ker would go off on mountain walks, over broad meadows strewn with Alpine flowers, or through the Dolomite valleys among waterfalls and rushing streams. In Freya's company, Ker appeared to lose much of his characteristic reticence and talked freely about his life and the history of literature which he loved.

'W.P. taught me the whole geography of Dante. He spoke and wrote about fifteen languages – none of the Oriental ones, but all northern European. He knew Anglo-Saxon, of course, and Middle-English, and being with him was like being near a magic well and knowing that even if you go on drawing and drawing from it for ever, it won't run dry. His company was a revelation and, to me, in those days, his knowledge seemed to encompass the whole of my world.'

'Yet the attraction must have been mutual,' I said.

'Oh, certainly. Although there was never a physical side. We were simply friends, wonderfully good friends. He'd been in love and had got engaged years before I met him; but his fiancée had died and he told me he'd never look in the same way at another woman.' She shrugged. 'Well, that was all right. We got on together marvellously in other ways and our friendship made us happy. What more. . . ?'

'Would you have described W.P. in those days as a contemporary sort of man, or not?'

'No, not really. I think most people thought of him as a rather eighteenth-century figure. He used to talk of literature as an idle pursuit; and while he was fully aware of action in the world he lived in, his attitude to books was that of an eighteenth-century gentleman of leisure.' She grinned. 'I remember him saying "All emphasis, all forcing of tone, is alien to polite literature."'

5

Men and Mountains

'I TAKE IT your friendship with your godfather didn't exclude other younger men.'

She shook her head vigorously. 'Oh, no! I didn't make dear W.P. an obsession, much though I adored him. No, no . . . war came along and I left Bedford College without taking my degree in English or history or whatever it might have been. I returned here to Asolo and trained for six months as a nurse at Bologna. Then I went up to a little hospital within sight of the front line guns and worked there until the war was over.

'Our little hospital was able to look after about a hundred men. To begin with, I was put on night duty; but it was no good. Nothing, not even war, could keep me awake. In the end, sister said, "This is not for you; better do your work during the day." So many years ago, and yet I can see things that happened as clearly as if it had been yesterday. . . .'

'What were you thinking about that made you say that?' I asked. 'Something to do with the hospital?'

'No, my dear, I was thinking of a train carrying soldiers either to or from where we were stationed. The train had stopped and we were sitting outside it, near the tracks, having some food. Suddenly a little aeroplane appeared above us – an enemy plane – and some of the men rushed back to the train for safety. The plane flew directly over and I saw the pilot reach out and drop a little package, actually it was a bomb, and then another. The bombs fell on to the carriage where the men had run and blew it to pieces. Can't think why the poor men ran to the train instead of remaining where they were, among the bushes near the line. . . .

'I remember the retreat at Caporetto . . . it was night. Our men had got down as far as they could, utterly exhausted, unable to take another step. I saw them all lying there; young men, lying among the white stones beside the river with the moon shining down on them. I dreamed about them sleeping in the moonlight, there among the stones, for months afterwards. . . .'

'There could hardly have been a greater contrast,' I said, 'strolling in the Dolomites discussing Dante with W.P. and so soon afterwards plunged into a war. You must have felt the waste and destruction terribly.'

'Yes, but there were the fine things, too! The young soldiers and their immense courage. The dream of victory. There was a wonderful spirit abroad . . . a spirit of real idealism. Great faith, love of country. Big, inspiring things! Kitchener asked for volunteers and got a million . . . every walk of life. The whole of Europe felt it.' She smiled. 'Even my own dear Papa, who had never told an untruth in his life, lied shamelessly about his age. Everybody wanted to do his bit for freedom.'

We finished talking about the war and I climbed downstairs through the trapdoor in the sitting-room floor, through the bedroom below, to the kitchen, where I made some tea. Freya remained where she was, leafing through her *Life History* scrapbook, which, she told me, she hadn't opened or looked at for years. After ten minutes or so, I went back upstairs with a tray of tea and biscuits and a few slices of freshly cut lemon in a saucer. I set down the tray, poured some tea and offered Freya a sugar-coated biscuit.

'You were going to tell me about what you were doing after the war.'

Freya bit off a corner from the biscuit. Munching slowly, she replied, 'I was just glancing through these pictures. . . . You see, there I am at our other house, L'Arma, bathing with

Vera's children, Paolo and Berto. Paolo has L'Arma now. . . . And then here, look: 1923, tramping with Venetia Buddicom in the Pyrénées. I look like Dick Whittington, don't you think, with that stick over my shoulder and our lunch wrapped in a scarf tied to one end of it!'

'I seem to remember either having read, or you telling me, that you were ill for a long time. But that might have been much later.'

'Yes. To begin with, I helped my mother run the silk-factory. It was useful, but fairly boring. A young man I'd been terribly in love with, actually engaged to, let me down and went off with an actress. I was miserable for a long time after that . . . I just couldn't get over it. Then things improved slowly, as usually happens, and life got back to normal.'

'I take it W.P. continued to visit you ever summer as before.'

'Indeed. But then, you see, he died. That was also in 1923 while we were climbing on Monte Rosa. It was all over quite suddenly. A few hours before, he had said to me, "You know, I've never been happier than I am now." Then, as we were going along, he gave a little cry and sank down and died. Rather wonderful way to go, happy and enjoying the scenery of your favourite peaks. He was buried at Macugnaga, below Monte Rosa. I used to visit his grave with a friend who, like me, is an Honorary Member of the Alpine Club. I think we're still the only two women members who don't have to pay. I certainly didn't deserve such a privilege, but they gave it to me anyhow. . . .' Freya sipped her tea. 'That reminds me, I must go to Macugnaga again . . . perhaps later on this year.'

'You still haven't explained about the illness. Do you think it was connected with your engagement, or might it have been a reaction to W.P.'s death? Or was there some other cause?'

'Really, I haven't the least idea. It was an ulcer and ulcers are commonly supposed to develop when a person is desperately worried, or overworked, or depressed about everything. Quite a lot had happened to me since I was thirteen. I'd been half killed; then there had been the war; then a broken engagement with lover disappearing; then my dear godfather dropping down on the mountain-side; and my parents' separation. Maybe the ulcer was my body crying out: "*Enough*!" Who knows?'

'Let's get back to mountains for a moment: this whole business of you as a climber interests me very much, since, until quite recently, I'd associated you always with the deserts of the Middle East – and Asia, of course.'

Freya replied quickly. 'Oh, but Mother and Father adored mountains! We were taken up every year when we were little; habit carried on. . . . From an early age, I began to feel a very close relationship with the great peaks. One might say, a great respect. The feeling was quite spiritual. Among mountains, I find always an atmosphere very like that of a cathedral. You're surrounded by every kind of space and yet none. Do you understand what I'm trying to explain?'

She drank more tea and continued. 'Getting up in the starlight and climbing through the night with your guides is a wonderful experience. We had to do this on the Matterhorn, before the sun melted the snow. Then there was Monte Rosa, which W.P. loved so much: different again. It's an ice-mountain and your steps have to be cut with an axe. A man would do his own cutting, of course, but being a woman, in those days guides cut all my steps for me. A tribute to Woman!'

'I'm not clear what you mean by describing the mountains as having a "spiritual atmosphere". I mean, I doubt if you're thinking in conventionally religious terms connected with Christianity.'

'No, you're quite right; I'm not. In any case, I don't attend church regularly. There are a good many points of dogma I can't truthfully accept, even in my own branch, the Church of England.'

'The Church of England. . . ?'

'Yes. . . . I daresay a little strange, since one's lived for so many years in a Roman Catholic country. Still, there it is. I was about to say, I feel an *affinity* with mountains, which may be the result of having been brought up for so much of my childhood within sight of them. I wouldn't be content to live for very long in flat country; any more than I would wish to end my days in a big city like Rome or London. Mountains inspire me always with a feeling of holiness. The Himalayan foothills gave me that sense when I first went there more than ten years ago. Rather like entering a church. It may be I feel like a pagan in church and like a Christian in the mountains. . . .'

'Was there any especially memorable experience that excited you, or was it just the mountain atmosphere as a whole?'

'The whole atmosphere, I think. Yes the whole. . . . I do remember, however, one marvellous experience I had in the Himalayas. My godson, with whom I'd been travelling, had gone off to look at the border of Tibet. I was rather tired by then and stayed behind. We'd reached a glorious place, looking up at Annapurna, the world's second highest; and I said: "I shall have my bed at the door of my tent and watch the sun go over Annapurna from sunrise to sunset."

'I fell fast asleep in the afternoon and woke at a great moment – the afternoon sun shining, absolutely nothing human there, just mountains and the sun. And quite spontaneously, the Resurrection came to me and that was the effect of the mountain and, I think, to me, the meaning of mountains as a whole.'

'There may be two ways of looking at this. On the one hand, there may be some force in the mountain atmosphere which works upon the climber's imagination. On the other, the person himself carries some spiritual element within him which mountains gradually reveal.'

Freya nodded briskly: 'Exactly what I mean when I talk about the effect of mountains! It's a feeling the mountain stirs up in you. Might be the acknowledgement of one's own existence. One's own spirit and the spirit of the little peak. . . . In any case we're all part of a greater spiritual body; just as our little finger is a part of ourselves. . . .' She held up her finger and waggled it. 'It has its own work to do, but it is also part of the greater machine.'

'This might explain why people who live their whole lives among mountains are supposed to be poetic and romantic.'

She raised an eyebrow: 'Well, my dear, I don't know what to say about that. I mean, in Nepal, for example, you find priests and lamas who spend their lives in what we think of as romantic places, but that's a matter of their religion. . . . Nearer to home, I don't believe for an instant that our Dolomite farmers are in the least bit poetic or romantic! They've a quiet-naturedness that may derive from the land and from spending so many hours each day with only oxen or horses for company. Doesn't imply necessarily that they're profound thinkers; but, I agree, they have a close relationship with their surroundings and a manner which one does tend to associate with mountains.'

I invited her to be more specific.

'Easier said than done, I'm afraid! I think it comes just from the quietness I speak of. Their eyes often have a sort of visionary look – clear and pale, used to great distances. You look into them and see there the vertical space and the lateral space and the mountain hardness. As if all their thoughts were conceived on a higher plane. . . . Perhaps these mountain peasant-farmers are like fallen gods, condemned to live forever in the shadow instead of at the summit of Parnassus!'

'Your talk of mountain gods makes me think of the English nature-writer, Richard Jeffries. Would you admit to feeling sensually about mountains in the same way Jeffries felt sensually about the earth?'

'No. Never. As I've already explained, we were brought up as children within sight of mountains, or carried through the valleys. For years and years, mountains themselves remained distant things with which I had no contact. Even later on, when I began to climb them, I can't recall having had sensual thoughts. . . .' She chuckled. 'Thoughts I had tended to be a trifle less prosaic!'

She added: 'Whenever I had climbed a peak, however, I would definitely think of it henceforth as mine and look proudly at it, towering in its range.'

'Just now, you dismissed the Dolomite farmers as unromantic figures, unaffected by the poetry of their mountain environment. I imagine your Alpine guides might have been different.'

'You mean in a romantic way? Well, not really, you know. They were all nice quiet men, but hardly what one would term romantic – except, to me, just a little, perhaps. . . ! The mountains may have lost the air of mystery for them; and yet, I'm certain that *wasn't* the case. But the guides had to know a great deal about them from a technical point of view. Like the whole of Nature, ourselves included, the mountains are constantly changing: solid rock gets fragile, due to the action of ice and water. What was once an easy way up, after a few years is classed as difficult. A mountaineer has to be conscious of these changes, or else his occupation becomes extremely dangerous.'

'But this completely contradicts the biblical simile which compares the immutable St Peter to a rock.'

'I think that's only because mountaineering hadn't got started then! Actually, climbing for sport goes back a good many centuries. . . . Petrarch was the first to write about it, wasn't he. . . ? Then we find the Alps being explored by English climbers. Remarkable what the early climbers achieved when you think of the equipment they had – or rather didn't have – compared to modern times.'

'Was your father a keen mountaineer? He had the right physique and temperament, after all.'

'Father was an excellent mountaineer. Surely I must have

told you about the time he and I got ourselves caught in a blizzard over there on Monte Grappa. . . ? Anyhow, snow was so thick that very soon the track became completely hidden. Father got us down safely by listening to the trickle of water under the melting snow and following its direction. That impressed me very much.'

'So water becomes a friend, not only in the desert, but among mountains for a different reason. . . .'

Her eyes glittered. 'Yes, that's right. To me, water is a friend. I can perfectly well understand how it might become an enemy but, as it happens, in the temperate zones of our world, water is liable to be a friend.'

'Your interest in mountains clearly goes back a long way.'

'Oh, indeed, it does. How I first got interested in mountain-climbing is quite complicated, when I sit here and try to work it out. My background . . . family . . . where we lived when I was little . . . people who would come and stay. All these had something to do with it. My dear godfather actually got me started on serious climbing. . . . When I went with Papa, we tended to walk rather than climb, I suppose.'

'In spite of all the modern refinements,' I said – 'equipment . . . improved techniques and so forth – it appears that the human factor is no less significant. Every year, one hears of more climbers being killed or badly injured.'

'Well, the risks are there and all part of the attraction. I believe quite firmly that life without risks of any sort would be a dull business. We need the awareness of death and a measure of risk to give life savour. I'm not for a moment suggesting that climbers or other people who practise an inherently dangerous form of sport deliberately take chances. But without the element of danger, climbing would become a far less interesting business. Danger and difficulty add up to challenge; challenge is what fires the imagination.'

'Have you ever been in a really tight spot?' I asked. 'I mean, with your life quite literally hanging by a thread.'

Freya smiled. 'As a matter of fact, your phrase, "hanging by a thread", would describe one little experience I had rather well. I happened to be climbing with some friends on the Roche Rouge . . . the exact year, I can't recall offhand. Anyhow, it doesn't matter. We were all roped together with a long strand between each person. Twenty metres, something like that.'

'Why such a distance?'

'Because very often it's hard for whoever is leading to find good rock; you know, firm enough to hold the belaying-pin. We'd got along fairly well and the others had all turned a corner without mishap. I was last in line. As I made to step aside, my foot slipped and I fell off the mountain. There was a terrific jerk as the rope went taut round my middle: then I started to swing backwards and forwards on the end of the rope, like a pendulum.

'All this went on out of sight of the others, who were safely round the corner. It was a strange sensation. . . . As I swung from side to side I saw how smooth the surface of the rock appeared. . . . I noticed tiny Alpine flowers – dianthus I think – growing in the crevices. I glanced down and saw a little flock of sheep grazing in a meadow far below me. Odd, isn't it, how clearly I can remember all these details!'

'If you had time to notice the rocks and the flowers and sheep, you must also have had time to wonder whether you'd be killed.'

'You know,' she replied, 'I tell you honestly, at that moment I wasn't the least bit frightened. I looked down into the valley and saw the sheep quietly grazing and I thought, "If the rope breaks and you fall, you'll die and that'll be that!" Just accepted death as a fact. Absolutely nothing whatever to be done about it. . . .'

'You must have been pretty badly shaken.'

'That certainly! The rope knocked all the wind out of me; couldn't have called for help, even if I'd wanted to. . . . Strangely enough, that didn't occur to me either. But the shock of the taut rope hurt a good deal, especially afterwards. Anyhow, the swinging motion slowed down by degrees. Then I managed to catch hold of the rock-face with my toe and pull myself up to safety. The others had no idea what had happened. I waited until we had all got back down to the little meadow and then I told them. Gave them quite a surprise!'

I wondered why she had abandoned Alpine climbing somewhere in the 1920s, after the Matterhorn expedition and Monte Rosa.

Freya shrugged. 'I suppose by then I'd found other things to do. . . . Poor Vera died, you see, and I looked after her children for a while on the Riviera. Then Viva Jeyes gave me Doughty's *Travels in Arabia Deserta*. I had intended it to last the whole summer – that must have been about 1924 . . . instead, I read it in a fortnight! From that moment Doughty tied me to the Arabs and I began to take Arabic lessons at San Remo from a little old monk. A year or two later, I spent the winter at Brumana, in Lebanon, up in the hills above Beirut – going on with Arabic. Then Venetia Buddicom arrived, I think on her way home from America, and together she and I explored the Jebel Druze in Syria. The French authorities weren't at all happy about us being there and gave us a lieutenant for protection. However, we soon managed to give him the slip and carried on. There wasn't any real danger – after all, what harm could two young English women on mules possibly do? After Syria, I got to Baghdad and started working for the *Times*, the local newspaper, that is; and then I wrote *Baghdad Sketches* and *The Valleys of the Assassins* and a whole new world began to open up in front of me.'

'I read Doughty's book again not long ago, although it took me longer than a fortnight to get through it. 1,400 pages, after all! I found that I liked it much better than before, but his Elizabethan style took a bit of getting used to.'

'From what point of view?'

'Well, to be frank, I'm not used to reading prose of that

sort every day and I found it slowed me down. To begin with, at any rate, I was conscious of actually having to read the words, rather than having the words flow through me. Does that make any sense?'

Freya considered briefly, hands folded on her lap. 'Odd you should say so. I must say, I've always thought that Doughty's Elizabethan prose fitted his subject perfectly. Didn't give me any trouble whatever. I see quite clearly what the problem was; but I'm puzzled why it should have been a problem. . . . Language has altered terribly much since my young day, of course; and it may be that I was more prepared for Doughty's mode of expression than you were. When we were children, our parents allowed us to read only the classics and good literature by Thackeray or Meredith . . . magazines were absolutely forbidden. That might have given me some advantage.'

'Anyway,' I said, 'it must have been more than Doughty's style that drew you to the world he'd described.'

'Oh, yes, much more. I realised suddenly what I wanted to do and where I would do it. I wanted desperately to travel in those ancient Middle Eastern lands; get to know them and their peoples, as Doughty had. The desert didn't particularly attract me, any more than I would be attracted to any sort of barren wilderness . . . you know, for its own sake. But I longed to discover Mankind's pathways and learn what had brought us down through history to where we are now. . . . It was these links with the past, along the great flowing river of history; these are what interest me most now – what drew me, utterly fascinated me, then.'

6

Journeys in Haggard Lands

THE EASTERN lands of imagination were places I had never known. Even so, it wasn't very difficult, listening to Freya talk, to picture myself on horseback, or aboard a camel, jolting across windswept plains towards ruined desert cities or remote encampments. Or, perhaps, reaching neither and lying down to sleep after sunset, beneath the desert stars. My penny-plain imaginings had been coloured by Freya's vivid descriptions of desert life as much as by her photographs: and yet still they lacked substance.

Here in the tower, above the calm Venetian plain, drinking lemon-tea and relaxing in a comfortable chair, the hardship of desert days – thirst, weariness, isolation – could not possibly be recreated with any degree of immediacy or truth. There could be no tactile awareness of what one great traveller had called the desert's 'harsh bite'. The images of its landscape, conjured up in words alone, were strangely bloodless and two-dimensional.

'And yet,' Freya mused, 'I wonder if you're entirely right about all that? You maintain that, because you've no first-hand experience of desert travel, what you picture in your mind can not be real. On the other hand, even although my recollections of the East are based on fact, I don't know that my imaginings are any more or less real than yours. Interesting philosophical question: what is real and what is not real? Not easy to answer. . . .'

'But think of the experience. It's something absolute you've acquired as a result of having travelled.'

'Well, is it, you see? I'm not so sure of that. Let me try to explain what I mean. Two people, travelling together along the same road, will receive very different impressions. The country through which they pass will have a different impact on each of them. So much depends on their individual interests, ability to perceive, understand what they see, and so forth. . . . Obviously, if a man is, for the sake of argument, a botanist, he is likely to get a different picture of the country from his companion who may be a geologist.'

'That sounds as if you're suggesting that specialised knowledge closes one's eyes as much as it opens them. As though it creates a kind of tunnel vision.'

'Not quite. I was trying, not very successfully perhaps, to emphasise that our own personal tastes and capabilities influence strongly the way in which we look at things. This becomes very clear when you write. The botanist and his geologist friend would probably each write quite differently about their journey. Shared experiences would not necessarily have equal significance for them. I don't suggest for a moment that their minds would be closed to everything except plants and rocks. By no means. But it would be strange if these interests did not influence each traveller's way of seeing landscape.'

'It's interesting to think of that in the context of modern expeditions – even quite modest ones – in which everybody is a specialist of some sort and highly qualified. In these days, when more expeditions are being mounted than ever before and, at the same time, far greater numbers of individuals travelling all over the world, I wonder if it's desirable for every traveller to be expert at something, or whether it's still enough merely to want to travel?'

'It depends very much what you mean by travel. There are so many sides to what you are implying. I think we might leave the scientific expedition out of it, since it's obvious that each of its members must have been chosen for the special qualifications he possesses. The same would apply, for instance, to mountaineering expeditions in the Himalayas.

'However, I think you are talking about the sort of serious travel that you as an individual might want to do; going off for weeks and months on end by yourself in a strange country, sleeping in a tent or a village, even trying to live off the land. Well then, of course some expertise and experience would be useful: for example, you would get on very much better with the people if you could speak a little of their language. You'd get far more out of the journey and, from a purely practical point of view, the journey itself would be made easier for you. Besides, I do think it's only polite to learn a few words of a language. Why else bother to go to the place? In any case, the people appreciate it, even if you don't pronounce the words quite correctly. The fact that you've made an effort is what counts. Speaking the native language gives you independence and a measure of control. You can be reasonably sure that your muleteer understands your wishes; you can ask at a village for a little food, or shelter for the night. Simple, useful things like that. You feel a part of your surroundings. Much nicer than feeling always distant and an outsider.'

'Of course, the twentieth-century package-tourist doesn't need to know any of these things, does he?'

'No, he doesn't. But the whole point of that sort of travel is to give people a glimpse of exotic places without the least bit of inconvenience to themselves. I've nothing against these tours, as such, and I'm sure they give many people pleasure. Personally, I don't like that way of travelling. I mean, just imagine, driving along in a bus, making light drawing-room conversation with your neighbours. The machine stops somewhere and you all get out for half-an-hour to watch local tribesmen dancing or people weaving baskets or beating copper or something. You're encouraged to buy awful little souvenirs. Everybody takes photographs. Then you all climb back into the bus and drive off somewhere else where the whole performance is repeated. I find this sort of travel utterly boring. I've done it once and I never want to do it again!

'Quite frankly, there's something terribly degrading and undignified about turning people and their ways of life into exhibits. It destroys the original meaning of their lives and whatever significance their occupations might have had. All right, the villagers earn a few dollars. But what happens? They become dependent on the tourism. The whole *raison d'être* of their traditional lives is gradually destroyed. I believe in preserving the natural diversity of races, but the idea of keeping traditional practices alive solely for the entertainment of foreign tourists horrifies and appals me. I see no justification for it, even on the most basic, materialistic grounds.

'There can always be found other ways of helping impoverished human beings, but to mummify traditional life, for the sake of it, goes against natural evolution. However much you may want to, you can't stop the flow of progress. There still are places on this beautiful earth where traditional life – in the sense of pastoral life – continues much as it did five hundred or a thousand years ago. I've visited these places often, by going on horses or mules, sometimes on foot. The people by now might have a few wireless sets, for all I know even television – though I doubt that! – but an awareness of the outside world brought by those means causes no discontent, nor curiosity sufficient to make them cast aside their traditions and go off to work as mechanics or labourers in the city. Thank goodness they don't or their lives would be miserable!'

'But what about Arabia? The vast changes that have been brought about by oil wealth? You couldn't possibly suggest that there has been much resistance to increasing material standards modelled on the West – redevelopment of the towns, cars, aeroplanes, European clothes.'

'Yes, it's a frightful mix-up. The Arabian situation is not quite what I had in mind, however. Enormous wealth has come so quickly to the sheikhs that change has accelerated out of all proportion. I was thinking more of the little mountain villages in eastern Turkey or the remote corners of Persia – I suppose I'd better say Iran – where the new materialism has come slowly like drops from a tap – not flooding everywhere like a burst dam, smashing and engulfing and carrying away whatever stands in its path. When change comes slowly, which is the natural way, it gets absorbed into whatever life it finds. A few restless spirits, usually young men needing money for a bride-price, might be drawn to the towns, but the old ways survive.'

'You're lucky to have been able to travel in the Middle East when it was still possible to share the traditional life of the nomads. In Arabia it's been abandoned all too quickly, don't you think?'

'No doubt about it. However, time alone will determine the extent to which we benefit or suffer. . . . It seems to me a tragedy that the rush of events in our modern world has gradually eliminated the spaces between them. . . .'

'I don't quite follow.'

'Well, let me give you an example. In the past, a man or a family would set out on a pilgrimage. They would walk and the journey would take a long time, weeks, maybe months. The destination was important, certainly, but the journey itself was the great thing. We've discussed such matters before. . . . They would meet strangers, sleep in strange places, hear the news, see unfamiliar sights.

'Nowadays, the majority of people who travel are interested only in the destination. They board an aeroplane and go to sleep while it rushes along above the clouds at hundreds of miles per hour. You don't see any detail of the ground below at thirty thousand feet; although, I must admit, the clouds can be very pretty at sunrise or sunset. But the real traveller still values the journey for its own sake, not simply as a means to an end. To the real traveller, the horizon is irresistible. I wrote about the horizon years ago somewhere; might have been in *Perseus in the Wind*. How did it go? ". . . that blue rim which stands between the known world and the unknown" . . . words to that effect.

'The bogus traveller, as I call him, has eliminated the skyline, just as he strives to eliminate all the unpredictable elements from his itinerary . . . takes all the fun out of it. Same little hotel-rooms, same food, same language. . . . Were these the only fruits of travel left to me in this world, I would far rather sit here in the garden in Asolo and remember happier days or read a book!'

'You would really give up travelling altogether?'

'Yes, I would.'

'But you'd be miserable, you know quite well you would. . . .'

'I expect that's so: but I dislike the thought of the alternative even more. Anyhow, I'll soon be dead and that'll solve everything. That's a journey I'm really looking forward to.'

'But why talk of dying when you're so in love with life and the world? Don't you feel there's so much you still want to see and do?'

She made a little calming gesture. 'You must try to remember, my dear, I am very, very old. . . . More than double your age. Of course I love travelling as much as ever, but now it's not so easy. I'm dreadfully slow and shaky on my feet . . . very apt to become ill . . . and worst of all, maddeningly forgetful. All these things. I'm always leaving my belongings behind in other people's houses. Sometimes I sit here and visualise the surface of the earth, thinly scattered with my possessions.' She chuckled. 'One becomes a burden to oneself and one's friends. Then it's time to go. Mind you, it's not quite over yet! After all, my dear doctor – such a nice man – was dead set against me going to Nepal last February. I told him that, at my age, in my state of health, with the prospect of only a few years left at most, the only right thing *was* for me to go back to the Himalayas. I said to him: "I'm putting three weeks of sheer delight against the possibility of three years of humdrum existence. If the journey's too much for me and I die in the mountains, what does it matter? At my age, be honest, what do three years matter more or less?"

'I don't want to write any more . . . don't want to take any more photographs. I tell you, I'd far rather die happily, like W.P., among the great peaks, than lie down there in my apartment, bed-ridden and unable to control my faculties. The dear doctor let me go.' She laughed impishly. 'Well, he didn't have much choice! Didn't approve at all, but didn't offer any more objections!'

I asked Freya how she pictured death and whether or not death, to her, had a tangible form.

'I don't know. . . . Perhaps I see death as a great bird – like an eagle – flying with outstretched wings. That's how I imagined death long ago and what I see now is not so very different. . . . Of course, it's hardly necessary to add that I speak now in strictly symbolic terms, as a direct answer to your question. The bird is just a pictorial invention. In fact, I don't believe that these images, real and unreal, which populate our lives, will carry over into the next world. If I think of the next world at all, I think of it . . . I mean, of myself . . . like a drop of rain falling into a mighty river which itself vanishes into the still mightier ocean. The tiny raindrop is a part of it all, but in no way identifiable.'

'To me, it's always tragic when somebody dies young, with whatever promise they might have shown largely unfulfilled. With respect, when a person dies at a great age, after a colourful, successful life, their death seems more readily acceptable.'

'Depends, doesn't it? Not everyone would agree upon what is meant by having a successful life. What might be success in the eyes of one, could equally well represent failure in the eyes of another. Unjust though it may appear, when we die is rather a matter of accident; to some extent beyond our control. Who's to know what we might or might not have achieved? You can hazard a guess, but really nobody can tell for certain. Still, I do agree, the fact they've been denied the opportunity to prove themselves is sad.'

For her own part, she admitted that she had few regrets. For example, it would have been exciting to have travelled more extensively in China, having first learned enough of the language to make conversation. She had gone there in 1961, but the trip had been very short and she had been unable to speak to anyone.

Spain also attracted her, particularly the south, where the Moorish influence could be seen and heard in the buildings and the everyday speech of the people. She had visited northern Spain briefly years ago, she said, and couldn't imagine why she had not returned. After all, it was so close to Italy; and although she did not speak Spanish, there were strong similarities between it and Italian. Getting about the country would be easy.

'If you decided to go to Spain tomorrow, how would you like to travel?'

'Ideally, I would like to ride a horse. Nothing too spirited, mind you! None of these wonderful Arabs would do . . . in any case, I don't think a thoroughbred would be suitable for jogging about the countryside. A rough little village pony would be best. One that knew how and where to find its food along the road.'

'You must read Penelope Chetwode's book, if you haven't read it already. It's called *Two Middle-aged Ladies in Andalusia*. The other middle-aged lady was her pony! It's enchanting, just what you have in mind.'

Freya made a note of the title. She laughed. 'It's really very exciting to think of so many journeys left to do. Also a little sad to know that one can't manage them all. One would need two lifetimes. . . .'

I asked Freya if there were any travellers of a particular period whom she especially admired; I added that I didn't necessarily mean travellers whose journeys or writings had influenced her own career directly.

'Are you thinking only of travellers in Arabia?'

'No . . . in general.'

She nodded slowly. 'General questions are apt to be difficult! I find it easier to think of a particular category.'

'In that case, let's take travellers in Arabia.'

She folded and unfolded her hands, concentrating hard.

'Difficult to say. Burton, for example, must have been interesting to know, but a disagreeable sort of character. Attracted to low life as much for its own sake as from intellectual curiosity. Undoubtedly brilliant. A kind of mad genius. . . . A great traveller? Oh, yes, no question about that. His obsession with sexual deviation I find unpalatable, somehow, but I daresay that sounds prim and old-fashioned. Quite apart from the moral aspect, I do see that Burton's tendency to linger in the dark alleys and *cul-de-sacs* of life may have added to his fascination in one sense, yet it has somehow also detracted from his greatness as an explorer . . . put him off course, if you like. I must say, his wife sounded awful! I read her biography years ago. Really a dreadful, bossy woman! I much prefer someone like the man who wrote *Eothen*. What was his name? Ah yes, Kinglake . . . Kinglake struck me as a sympathetic person. I have the first edition in the apartment . . . well over a hundred years old, with a coloured frontispiece. He captured the spirit of the East, don't you agree?'

'Certainly. But then so did Burton.'

'Such a long time since I read any of his books . . . *The Pilgrimage to Mecca* and *First Footsteps*. I wouldn't like to judge, except that I don't remember Burton's writing having the poetry of Kinglake's.'

'All right. What about T. E. Lawrence? Surely there's enough poetry for you in *The Seven Pillars*?'

Freya beamed. 'Oh, yes . . . a wonderful book! An immense, sustained effort . . . very poetic . . . full of authentic atmosphere. Only, I feel that Lawrence's ego kept getting in the way of his work. The *Crusader Castles*, for example: a remarkable achievement without a doubt, yet somehow an achievement flawed by Lawrence's preoccupation with being first in the field. He must have known that Frederick Walpole had written an excellent book about the Lebanon in the nineteenth century. I don't understand this aspect of Lawrence. He was so concerned with his effect on other people. Now that's odd for somebody who is really involved with his own work. . . .'

'Accepting what you say, I'd always contend that Lawrence's extraordinary ability far outweighed the blemishes in his character.'

'Certainly he had great possibilities – even genius. I don't know what to think about his career, however, had it gone on.' Freya paused, the train of thought exhausted.

I said: 'People have criticised Lawrence's desire to seek anonymity in the ranks of one Service or another: first in the Tank Corps; then the Royal Air Force. Do you believe his search was genuine, or, to put it bluntly, was it simply a means of attracting attention to himself? In other words, a stunt. . . .'

Her features glowed with passion. 'Absolutely not! To me it's dreadful that poor Lawrence should have been considered a publicity-monger, or even demented, for vanishing into his temporary obscurity. It seems to me quite natural that such a highly strung, gifted man should have sought peace and quiet and some relief from his burden of responsibility, after all he'd been through with the Arabs in the Desert War. The war must have drained his energies; well, in fact, we know that it nearly killed him. He was very far from being mad . . . needed simply to get away from it all.

'It's inevitable, I suppose, but a pity nevertheless, that Lawrence's highly exceptional life has been judged so frequently by men who have themselves led rather ordinary lives. They're just not equipped to understand the pressures he was subjected to. Anyone who had come through the Desert War . . . anyone who had lived for any length of time with the desert Arabs, would understand some of these pressures. I find Lawrence's post-war behaviour perfectly comprehensible!

'But I'm still undecided to this day whether or not *The Seven Pillars of Wisdom* attracts such overwhelming attention because of its subject-matter, and whether the force of the book as literature transcends this. . . . It's a great shame: I'd planned to meet Lawrence during 1935, the year he was killed.'

I reflected that, for the second time within a few years, she had been robbed of the opportunity of knowing another European whose exceptional talents, like her own, had found their ultimate expression in the Arab world: the first, Gertrude Bell, who had died in Baghdad in 1926, then Lawrence. I said:

'I think it's really infuriating that so many writers after Aldington have concentrated so much effort upon exposing defects in Lawrence's character and sensationalising events like the assault on him by Turkish soldiers at Dera. It seems to me that these revelations have done little else except surround Lawrence's character with an aura of increasing disrepute . . . a reputation which I believe to be largely undeserved.'

Freya bit her lip and nodded. Her expression became suddenly sad and when she replied, her voice was filled with melancholy. 'Ah, but don't you also feel that this is a very bad time for literature? So much that is written now seems to me a self-conscious attempt at being clever for cleverness's sake. The passion for advertisement has led to many things being written, not for their own sake, but – very often – with a view to making money or a reputation. The quieter virtues which drew me to my craft still find true responses in the world, but the juggernaut of advertisement is a terrible leveller and the enemy of serious writing.'

'But then, there are many of Lawrence's biographers who would insist that advertisement, I mean by that *self*-advertisement, had been a primary motive in his own life. The adoption of Arab dress, the mystique woven about his desert adventures, his ostentatious retreat into the limelight of obscurity . . . would you *utterly* reject all such criticisms?'

'Oh, reject them without question! Now, look here; there's nothing whatever wrong with wearing Arab clothes *when one is in Arabia*. Besides, Lawrence already spoke Arabic, although according to his own modest admission, and the evidence of those who knew him, he spoke it rather badly. The Arab dress made him, if anything, *less* conspicuous; many other Englishmen in the East have done the same. Much of the mystique, as you term it, was pure, romantic twaddle, fabricated by Lowell Thomas. . . . As for Lawrence retreating into the limelight; well, you know what I think of that . . . complete nonsense! However, let me say again: in Lawrence, we have a sensitive, highly responsive person; brave, extremely gifted. I grant you, he did allow too much rein for his ego. But he must be seen, after all, as an artist and a poet as well as a soldier and a historian.

'I honestly wonder how his critics who have never set foot in Arabia, never experienced any sort of hardship or risk, would have reacted to the Desert War . . . in particular to the type of close-range, guerrilla-warfare which Lawrence himself engaged in, blowing up trains, that sort of thing. I'm not the least bit surprised that afterwards he wanted to get away from it all for a while . . . let somebody else take decisions for him. It's quite natural. How he went about it is, perhaps, not entirely above criticism, but, then, which of us leads a perfectly blameless life? Nearly every day we do something ill-advised or mistaken . . . it's a part of the human condition!' Freya laughed and glanced about her. 'If that weren't so, why then we should all be gods!'

'Anyhow, I'm pretty sure you wouldn't quarrel with Lawrence's literary judgement. He did, after all, manage to get Doughty's *Arabia Deserta* republished.'

Freya's face immediately brightened. 'Yes, and what a marvellous introduction he wrote to that edition! Alas, I've not read it for years. . . .' She smiled affectionately. 'Dear old Doughty! He was *the* man so far as I'm concerned. It was his *Deserta* that tied me to the Arab world for good. Altogether a wonderful piece of work. You complain that the style is difficult, but, to me, it's enchanting and exceptionally well suited to the subject. Again, there was a man who travelled his own road . . . listened to the voice of his own conscience.'

'I find it interesting that Doughty's travels, like the *Arabia Deserta* itself, were in reality mere stepping-stones towards the poetry which he'd meant to write later . . . *Dawn in Britain*, *Mansoul*, all that.'

'Yes, so do I. Rather like the travels and discoveries of Burckhardt years earlier. Remarkable to think of discoveries, such as Petra and the Temple of Rameses at Abu Simbel, being merely incidentals during his years of preparation for the great exploration of the Sahara. . . .'

'Which he never accomplished. . . .'

'No. . . .' Freya smiled sadly. 'Poor Burckhardt! Died in a Cairo slum when he was only thirty-two. I think he must have been one of the most outstanding, you know. . . . He and Doughty I would put together.'

'What about mere modern Arabian travellers?'

'Jack Philby was the only one I really knew well. He was brave and kind and the Arabs loved him . . . a dear, true friend. Funny, but I find his books ever so slightly dull. *The Empty Quarter*, for instance. The story of his journey and the events are thrilling, but for some reason the actual writing falls awfully flat. I don't know quite why that should have been, do you?'

'I've only read *The Empty Quarter* and I don't know any of Philby's other writing. It's true enough what you say. It does read a bit flat. I didn't mind that very much because it seemed to me that the spareness of the writing reflected the hard desert environment. Got the feeling of the desert across. I wouldn't hold it up as a work of great literature as such, but I do think it succeeds as a chronicle of an epic journey. Actually, I'd much rather have it written like that . . . economical, even a bit barren. Bertram Thomas, for example, is marvellously good, but here and there he takes off in flights of technicolour prose which, to be frank, I don't like.'

'Oh, dear, this has a familiar ring! But surely it's just as bad if a book is all underwritten or is all purple passages? It's a matter, isn't it, of striking a happy medium? The writing needs to be tuned, like an instrument. No, we can do better than that: what I mean to say is, a book, having got started, goes trotting off, rather like a horse. And sometimes it needs to gallop, other times it needs to stand still. The writer has to see this and realise it. That is what makes the difference.'

'I've sometimes heard your own work criticised for its purple passages. Do you think that's fair or not?'

She laughed. 'I'm quite sure I've told you before how Jock Murray used to complain about little passages here and there which he felt I ought to tone down. In many instances, he would be quite right and I would submit. But, at other times, I didn't agree and then I would think, "Well, I know a little bit about my trade, after all, and they seem fine." Dear Jock wasn't always very pleased with me!'

'Keeping to Arabia and *The Empty Quarter* – what's your opinion of Wilfred Thesiger's work?'

'I have two of his books at the flat: *Arabian Sands* and *The Marsh Arabs*. They're both beautifully written. I think he's by far the best of all the modern writers on Arabian travel.'

'That's high praise, coming from another Arabist.'

'Well, you see,' she said, 'he's done these journeys, like Philby and Thomas. He's also been able to write about them. No mean feat being able to bring readers with you through a landscape where only a handful have managed to go. He must be sad to think of all that's happened in Arabia since oil got started.'

I told her that Thesiger now spent most of each year in

northern Kenya and that he felt depressed about the thousands of tourists flocking there annually. Problem was where else to go.'

Freya said she could understand perfectly Thesiger's feelings about crowds, especially tourists. Embracing the surrounding landscape with the sweep of an arm, she remarked how Asolo had once been so quiet, the streets quite empty except for a few donkeys or ponies or a handful of passers-by.

'Listen now and you'll hear nothing but the noise of motor-bicycles and cars. Their engines drown the birdsong. Awful things!' She admitted that she used to drive a car, but had given it up about twelve years ago; as she put it, mercifully before she had killed somebody! She went on: 'Look how the countryside has been built up. The authorities here are very strict, I'm glad to say . . . you can't put up just anything. But even so I look out at all these cars and the rash of villas spreading over our hills where a few years ago there were none, and I feel it's all rather a shame.'

'Hearing Thesiger say that is one thing, but aren't you now contradicting a view you've often expressed before about accepting change as inevitable, for better or worse?'

'Ah, well, that may be,' she answered. 'However, having stated that change is an essential part of life, I don't mean to say we should sanction change merely for the sake of it. What I'm driving at simply is that it's wrong – and I think a little naïve – to oppose the principle that the whole course of life must embody change, as it goes on. Whether change is good or bad and whether you view it as progressive or retrogressive is relative and a temporary matter . . . down to individual conscience. It's the unalterable *fact* of change we have to come to terms with, in my opinion. No good turning our backs on it. But we should all try, as far as we're able, to ensure that change assists the spiritual as well as material well-being of our age.'

7

Love and Marriage

'MARRIAGE is such a complicated affair,' Freya sighed.

We had been discussing a mutual acquaintance and now the conversation began to turn back upon ourselves. 'It affects people in so many different ways. It's refreshing to meet a couple who are so totally devoted to each other. . . .

'Politeness in married life is vital; of that I feel sure. I know a good many people who don't have much of the physical side of the relationship, but who are good companions and devoted and true friends. This would have been enough for me always, if the other were impossible.'

'I find it hard to imagine that companionship would have been enough when you were young. Although I do see that it might be acceptable to someone much older.'

Freya nodded. 'Of course, it would be agreeable to think of both coming together. When I was a girl, no doubt I dreamed of such things, but, looking back, if dear W.P. had asked me to be his platonic companion, I would have gone to live with him willingly. It would have been enough to be always near him, sharing his wonderful conversation. The physical side wouldn't have mattered to me in the least. Our companionship and good friendship were indeed enough.'

'Don't you feel that a marriage based entirely on companionship might have been in the long run rather unsatisfactory; the prose of love rather than the poetry? Are you quite certain that you wouldn't have felt cheated?'

'Well, I must say, I'd rather have good prose than bad poetry any day!'

In a more serious vein, she added: 'You must remember, in any case, that the physical side of marriage doesn't go on indefinitely. To take the other extreme: a marriage based on nothing but sex must be doomed, if only for biological reasons. Besides, you cannot be *continuously* involved with sex; so what happens in between? The intellectual life of a marriage is important. Also, I think each of the partners ought to have the freedom to continue with his or her own life. I am sure that such freedom is just as essential as being together and it may well be that the denial of it causes more unhappiness and frustration than anything else.'

'Are these merely thoughts, Freya; or are you speaking also from personal experience?'

'Yes, of course my own experience comes into this. Our poor little marriage was not a happy one, as you know. Before we married, S. was kind and gentle, a very genial companion. Afterwards, the whole thing changed . . . not very reassuring when your life-partner appears so evidently pleased every time he has to leave you!'

'Why did you marry him?' I asked.

'I didn't know him as well before as I did afterwards! I think that was the reason.' She sighed.

We sat in silence for several minutes before Freya picked up the thread again.

'After we married, S. changed completely. He resented the fact that people liked me. I had a great many acquaintances and many good friends. I think I was generally popular – besides, I've never been the sort of person who drops friendships after they've been made. It's fair to say that my books had been quite successful and I had done journeys which had gained me recognition. Poor S., I'm sure, felt out of it . . . goodness knows why. Success and all that has never meant very much to me.'

'One thinks of you immediately as a warm, affectionate person. Yet, from what you say, these were the very qualities lacking in your marriage.'

'If we gave a dinner-party and I happened to be talking to our friends at my end of the table, S. would fall completely silent. Couldn't bear it. . . . I do believe that I made an effort; however' – her eyes twinkled – 'as a friend once put it, "It takes two to make a marriage and sometimes three!" That's a quotation from somebody; can't remember who.'

She went on: 'No, you see, there was never any real feeling of sharing. Towards the end, he hardly even spoke. I'd have liked it to remain as friendship. . . . Used to write, but he never answered.'

'You honestly believed friendship was still possible and worth striving for?'

'Oh, yes, most certainly. Marriage is difficult though. I've often wondered whether a series of happy short relationships wouldn't be preferable; each of them ending – no, I mean continuing – as a friendship. That would be a very pleasant way to live.'

It sounded almost priggish when I said: 'But then what about children and family life? You need something more permanent, surely, if you want to have children.'

'Quite true. But nowadays there are far too many people in the world. The object should be to limit population, not to increase it. The concept of the large Victorian family is out of date. Marriage and the marriage vows are there with procreation in mind and the preservation of the legitimate family circle. That's all very well, but we have reached a situation where, if people continue to produce large numbers of children, the effect upon the world's resources will be catastrophic.'

Freya repeated her earlier remarks about children. She said she liked them, but preferably in small doses. Otherwise she found them rather trying. She had never felt that women should be regarded primarily as housewives and producers of offspring. Such a role was too limiting: fulfilling, admittedly, for some, but desperately frustrating for others. The conversation had taken a more general turn and she looked relieved to have done with talking of her own marriage.

She leaned forward conspiratorially. 'It would be fascinating to make a study of marriage customs in different countries. Find out how circumstances compare. For instance, I've often thought that there's something to be said for the custom of arranged marriages; especially if you have kind, loving parents who take pleasure in seeing you happy. They would take infinite trouble to find just the right man and, of course, all the practical matters such as money and possessions would be settled amicably between the two families. It seems such a pity when young people are forced to start from scratch with few, if any, of these desirable advantages. I have heard it said that having to struggle to make ends meet in the early days strengthens the marriage ties, but I don't quite swallow that argument . . . there's no virtue in cultivating hardship for its own sake.

'Then there's the Muslim practice of keeping more than one wife. Even as a mere woman, I can quite see how it must be pleasant for a man to wander from one wife to the next. Still, it must call for great tact on the husband's part, otherwise life could become very tricky. I once asked a sheikh what he thought of it all and he replied that, indeed, it was very nice, except that instead of buying just one pair of silk stockings, or whatever, he had to buy sixteen. *Imagine!*

'I think it was twice in the course of their history that Greek kings and powerful nobility checked the growth of population by forbidding anybody to have children. It shows that such things are possible. I can't remember offhand where I read this, but I do know that I'd never heard of it before. But, you know, going back to our earlier conversation, I honestly believe that I would rather have had a happy friendship than a conventional marriage with the physical side ungenerously given. It isn't that I was excessively demanding in those days. Quality, not quantity, is the great thing.'

'Take the sheikh and his sixteen wives. He can't possibly care for each wife equally. He must have favourites. It's human nature. But it does seem a bit hard on the less-favoured wives.'

'It probably is,' Freya replied. 'Still, that is the system and the women are ready to accept it. There may be some reaction against it nowadays in the cities, among students, for example. But generally speaking the custom of polygamy is accepted unquestioningly throughout the Muslim world. I remember a few years ago visiting another old sheikh in his tent in the Syrian desert. He kept me sitting talking in an armchair from seven in the evening until two the next morning, when our dinner was eventually brought in. The rest of my little party had managed to curl up and go to sleep in various corners of the tent, but I was obliged to sit there in the middle of it all until the food came! Anyhow, some months later, the old sheikh arrived in London where I also happened to be, and we gave a little dinner-party for him by way of thanks. The sheikh turned up with one of his wives and – would you believe it? – two little girls he'd picked up on the doorstep of the Dorchester! I must say, the friends I was staying with took it all very calmly. I give them full marks for that.

'I hardly knew what to talk to the girls about, but in the end I asked one of them where she came from and what it was like. She was slender and fair-haired with rather a hard little face, but almost immediately her expression softened and she began to describe her upbringing in Wales. She was happy talking about the countryside and it was wonderful to watch the change in her manner as she spoke. I find that most people enjoy talking about their homes, a useful subject to bear in mind when you're travelling abroad.'

I wondered whether Freya thought that her story had a moral.

She smiled. 'Don't you think it's an immoral rather than a moral tale? I mean, picture the wicked old sheikh and his poor, long-suffering wife and these hard-faced girls from the Dorchester steps! Quite extraordinary altogether! It goes without saying that a European wife wouldn't have stood it!

'Yet that poor little Muslim wife would calmly bear her husband's follies, disliking them, I feel quite sure, every bit as much as you or I would, but accepting them as an inevitable part of her daily life. I think life with that wicked old man must have been particularly hard.'

'It must be difficult for women in Arabia when they grow old and find themselves being replaced by younger wives with better looks.'

'Oh, very. I remember staying the night in someone's house in the Hadhramaut, or it might have been Yemen, and a very nice wife showed me her little room, quite tiny, with a rather dull view and so on. And then the poor creature told me that, having started off as number one, she was now number four and as she descended the scale her room became smaller and smaller. . . . I felt very sorry for her: such a nice woman.'

Freya went on: 'Arabia can be an awkward place for females . . . English women, too. A great chum of mine got ill and was convalescing with some Arab friends. There she was in bed one day, when a holy woman came in. Some other women had made coffee and one passed a cup to Doreen, handing it first of all to the holy woman who spat into it as a blessing! Poor Doreen had to drink the contents, spit and all . . . couldn't possibly have refused. Shows what we women sometimes have to do!'

'That's gruesome; but it does make one look at travellers like you and Gertrude Bell with different eyes. . . . As a matter of interest, I've often wondered how you and she would have got on, had you been able to meet.'

Freya said she would have liked to meet Gertrude Bell very much, but doubted whether they would have become friends. 'You see, Gertrude had the reputation of being very hard on other women Arabists. Liked to keep her own little world to herself. She was Oriental Secretary but, towards the end of her life, became unpopular and I was told that she didn't receive the official papers she required to do her work because nobody wanted her involved. She must have been an exceptionally gifted woman, nevertheless. I've read her books, of course, and admire them . . . *Amurath to Amurath* and *The Desert and the Sown* . . . superb writing.'

'Gertrude Bell's standards as a writer and traveller must have given you a target to aim for, in your early days in Baghdad.'

'Travels certainly: but I don't think her writing influenced mine. Indirectly perhaps. There are so many influences on one's work one isn't remotely aware of.'

I asked Freya whether as a young woman in Iraq, she had made any conscious effort to follow in Gertrude Bell's footsteps. She shook her head. I added by way of mitigation: 'I know people are always searching for comparisons between travellers or writers. I don't believe it's possible to compare people. It's really a waste of time and yet here I am asking the same old question. . . .'

'Well, there are far worse crimes, believe me! No matter, I agree with you, such comparisons are usually pointless. . . . Periods of history, individual circumstances and personalities differ so.'

'I wonder whether in a marriage the differences you speak of are a strengthening or a weakening force?'

'What can I say? This question is so like many others one hears in conversation. . . . If we take a concrete example, then it might be possible to reach a definite conclusion. As a general question, I don't think it makes sense.'

'What about your own marriage, then? You and your husband clearly had completely different personalities. Did these differences help or hinder your relationship?'

'Hindered it,' she replied serenely. 'I have no hesitation in saying that.'

'Just suppose your marriage had been blissfully happy but that your husband had urged you to give up travelling, say altogether. Let's assume he had been loving and attentive

. . . really hated the idea of you being away from home. What would you have done?'

'Oh, I think I would have tried to please him. But, you see, one ought really to avoid getting into such an awkward predicament. There is a practical side to marriage, as there is to the rest of one's life, which must be dealt with. The two partners should be able to discuss their financial affairs quite openly, get them straight and then forget about them. Likewise, it's a grave mistake to abandon all one's interests, one's little bit of territory, even for the sake of someone you love dearly. If it's true love, not simply infatuation, there should be no difficulty about this. But if there is a difficulty, then perhaps something is fundamentally wrong. Over-possessiveness, for instance, is as bad as disinterest.'

She continued. 'It's rather like having a garden. Ignore what grows there and sooner or later things will die. Conversely, drown everything with water and bury plants in fertiliser, fuss over the wretched things day in and day out, and you stand an equally good chance of killing them. Both are extremes. People are no different; we all need space to move about in and air to breathe as much as we need love, friendship and reassurance. The art lies in finding the right balance; too little of one is as fatal as too much of another.'

Freya disagreed completely with the theory that marriage had to be worked at, like any other job, to be successful. She maintained instead that it should be easy, a pleasant sort of experience; not, as she put it, a life-sentence with hard labour. I reminded her of her writing; of the months and years of hard work she had devoted to making her beautiful, seamless prose. It seemed reasonable to suppose that a marriage, in order to run smoothly, might demand the same dedication.

She would have none of it. 'You must realise that writing books and being married are two rather different things. I have had a little experience of both, after all. . . . Perhaps one might say this: when you are writing a book the idea of the book is always with you. It becomes a part of your life, even if you are not actually sitting at your desk or even thinking about it particularly . . . it's simply *there*. Marriage should be the same, an easy companion or, if you like, an easy condition. When difficult moments come, you carry on as usual, working steadily through them. Neither occupation ought to hang round your neck like a mill-stone. Some people worry that their lives have become routine and complain the spark has gone out of living. Well, there's absolutely nothing wrong with having a routine. What I suspect they are really suffering from is apathy, which is something else entirely. Still, as long as the marriage partners remain good friends and aware of each other, the risk of apathy destroying their world is not very great.'

'It sounds to me as if you're really agreeing after all that one must work at marriage to keep it going.'

'I stand by what I said earlier,' she replied determinedly. 'In marriage one should have an easy , relaxed feeling. I admit that any worthwhile relationshop, like any worthwhile possession, should be looked after . . . naturally I must include marriage in that. . . . But in the business of looking after, you have to be extremely careful not to stifle or smother the delicate freedom of it all. Rather like holding a bird in your hand. . . . no matter how beautiful it might be, you must always be ready to let it go. After all, it is the nature of the bird to fly.'

'Just as it's part of your nature to want to travel and discover new horizons?'

'Yes, yes!' She looked me in the eye. 'Actually, I must be honest and confess I would be very unhappy to think that I could never pack a bag when I wanted to and set off somewhere, ever again. I daresay I would have abandoned all that for love, but, there again, surely anyone who truly cared would not prevent one from doing just a few of the things one likes?'

8

People and Books

APROPOS of nothing, it seemed, Freya drew my attention to a shaft of sunlight playing on the pink silk cushions and projecting shifting patterns of foliage on to the sitting-room sofa.

She remarked that the sunlight reminded her of illustrations in a book she had read as a child. 'Makes me think of Joan of Arc, who was my heroine. If I'd been very good, Mother would say, "Tomorrow you can be Joan for a day." I loved that! I've still got the book about Joan somewhere . . . it was by a French author.'

'Curiously enough, I came across it a few days ago,' I said. 'It's in the cupboard where you keep duplicate copies of your own books. It's got purple covers with gold lettering.'

'Yes, that's it.'

'There are lots of other old books there as well,' I said. 'I was hunting for *Rome on the Euphrates* and eventually found it among them.'

Freya laughed. 'Another example of my technique for mislaying possessions! It's a miracle if anything turns up! You say other old books are there too. . . . Do you happen to remember what they were?'

They were mostly novels by nineteenth-century authors: Scott, Thackeray, Jane Austen, the Brontë sisters, Dickens, Meredith and Stevenson. There was some poetry by Wordsworth, Milton and Browning; and one or two books by George Borrow, which Freya told me had belonged to her father.

'Papa was very fond of Borrow,' she said. 'I think his favourite of all was *The Bible in Spain*: he was always getting that down from the shelf and going off with it. We had several others – the Welsh journey and the gypsy volumes, *Lavengro* and *Romany Rye*. I'm not sure why father liked *Bible in Spain* . . . perhaps it had something to do with a little expedition he'd made as a young man, when he rode along the southern coast as far as Granada.'

'I've a feeling that you don't share your father's taste for Borrow. . . .'

'Actually, I don't care that much for his writing! He's inclined to be too dogmatic . . . always having little contests about languages. Would have been a rather heavy companion for a long journey.

'You know, thinking of St Joan, whom I felt I really knew, as a child . . . I've known a good many writers over the years and yet many of my favourites, like George Meredith, I never met, nor indeed could have. Yet they feel like old friends. Very curious, this bond one feels with certain writers' work. Wordsworth, for instance: I've wished often that I could have met him.'

'According to some biographies, he tended to be rather stern and withdrawn; aloof, might be more accurate.'

'Well, people find all sorts of different things. Although it's much too vague to say simply *people*.' Her tone hardened. 'At least, Wordsworth always would have had something to say. He had a true eye . . . really true eye. Vast imagination. . . .' She began to quote, instinctively, from Wordsworth's perhaps most famous poem:

' "For oft, when on my couch I lie
In vacant or in pensive mood,
They flash upon that inward eye
Which is the bliss of solitude. . . ." '

She smiled. 'That makes me think of the slopes above

Marostica, on the road to Vicenza. Slopes all covered with snow-white cherry blossom. I feel about the cherry blossom what I imagine Wordsworth might have felt about his daffodils.' She completed the quotation:

' "And then my heart with pleasure fills,
And dances with the daffodils." '

'I find similarities between Wordsworth and your godfather, W.P. Both were fastidious about the use of words; both had a grave and serious air. Have you ever seen them as kindred spirits?'

Freya acknowledged that similarities might have existed between the two men and that they shared a view of the English language which she herself upheld: the virtue of good language and the absolute necessity of choosing words which express exactly the writer's meaning.

'W.P. used to say that, in literature, one had to be clear first of all oneself about what one wanted to say. If it was a matter of describing an object, such as a vase, or a stretch of country, or the expression on a person's face, you had to decide just what it was you wished to convey . . . then find the word or a phrase that did it. I think Wordsworth would have approached his work in this way. No one abused language less than he. No one has had a greater feeling for what is apt.'

'Time and time again, when discussing writing as a craft, you've denounced much of our present-day literature. Yet, when talking about the nineteenth century, you single out writers like Thackeray or Jane Austen or the Brontës. Perhaps one tends to forget that there were dozens of bad writers churning out rubbish then, too.'

She chuckled. 'Oh, certainly! We have to compare like with like, or there's no basis for comparison. When we talked about this a few days ago, I was thinking of writers who have a reputation, not third-rate journalists or the sort of people who reel off sickly romance by the gross. The fact is, however, not many of our living authors have that timelessness in their work that Jane Austen managed to achieve. All right, details of life have changed: we don't travel about in carriages and nowadays houses are lit by electricity; but the basic facts of life and character go on, and it's in portraying these she succeeds so magnificently.

'I'm convinced that much of her timeless quality is due to the use of language; language which is essentially good English, well constructed and used to portray living men and women. Actually, her language is so good that you're not aware of it. A bit like having good clothes: if they're really well tailored and fit, rather than cheap and outrageous, you don't pay particular attention to them except to be aware of a sense of excellence. They don't distract your attention from the person who's wearing them and who should be, after all, a little more important.'

'I would think of clothes more in terms of wrappings; whereas words are like the painter's colours: anyhow, a vehicle for expression rather than a container of it.'

Freya nodded. 'Or indeed both. I'm trying to get across what I mean by the seemliness of language. These writers of one or two centuries ago used our language superbly. A good test is to try to decide which book you would take with you on a long journey. Quite obviously, inferior writing and superficial material would pall very quickly. A little must go a long way on a journey. A traveller needs something much deeper that doesn't date. You want to be able to read a few lines and have something to occupy you for the rest of the day, as you jog along on your mule or tramp through whatever new landscape it is.

'I used to take Virgil, whose verses didn't need much room in a saddle-bag, whose language I love and whose wonderful, soothing dreams of earth helped me through many difficulties. Virgil would provide me with a line or two for daily contemplation and, being written in Latin, the little extra pleasure of making the best translation I could.'

'Why is it that we very often bring a book completely unconnected with the country we're travelling in: perhaps an old childhood favourite, or even a book we would probably not be drawn to at home?'

'Hard to say,' Freya answered. 'For my own part, I do tend to carry a book or books which I would just as happily read here. Virgil is a case in point: the same would apply to any of the other Greek or Latin authors on my shelves. It might be that we need some little token of familiarity in a strange country. Otherwise, I find it best to do any reading about a new country here, at home, and keep my mind free to receive impressions of it as I go along.'

'You told me a year or two ago that you were working your way gradually through the Roman writers. I noticed a book about Sir Francis Drake lying open on the table when I arrived and I'd meant to ask whether you've now finished with the Romans, or whether Drake was merely an interlude.'

Freya grinned. 'Coming up for breath, so to speak! I admit, it felt like that sometimes among my dear Romans! As you know, I arranged my books ages ago, so that the Sumerians came first, on one shelf; then the Cretans; then Egyptians, Greeks, Romans and so forth. My plan has been to read through all these in sequence so as to see the whole of our history and the lines that come down to where we are, from the beginnings of time. . . . Not much to do, is it?' She grinned again. 'I have to confess that I liked the Romans less than the Greeks. Difficult to say exactly why . . . the Romans had this insatiable desire to conquer and possess. Why, for example, they wanted to come to England, when they had all the lands they needed in Europe and elsewhere, I'm at a loss to understand. The climate was poor in England and the tribes were hostile . . . a long way off from Rome . . . very strange. The Greeks were gentler and I think more civilised.'

'This means, I take it, that you didn't finish all the Roman volumes?'

'I'm afraid not. Gave up somewhere about the half-way stage and went on to read about the Crusades. It's not the right attitude for a scholar, but after all I am eighty-nine and at the present rate of progress, I doubt if I'll finish reading them all. . . . It makes me a little sad to think of all these books scattered about my flat and here, in the tower; books which I'll never read again.'

'At one point in his life, W.H. Auden, I'm told, used to visit friends' houses and go immediately to the bookshelves to see whether they had some work or other of his own which he wanted to read: apparently, he used to read his own poetry and so on, rather than anybody else's writing; and if a friend didn't have the book, Auden would be quite annoyed and say, "You really ought to have it" or, "I can't imagine why it isn't here". You don't talk very much about your books and I've hardly ever seen you reading one.'

'Well, it's true certainly that at one stage Auden did probably live too much inside himself and his own world. . . .' Freya glanced about the sitting-room. 'None of my own books is up here at all at the moment, except those you're working from perhaps. No, it's odd; I don't read books of my own very often, although now and then I'll go back and look at one, sometimes, with pleasure and even a little surprise; other times, wondering why I wrote something in that way. . . . For example, I glanced the other day at *The Lycian Shore* and put it down convinced that the early chapters would be best omitted altogether, if it were ever to be reprinted. They're not particularly good – all right, I suppose; I can never tell – but they interfere with the book getting started.'

I asked her if she had any special favourites; or come to that, were there any of the books which she considered had failed to meet her exacting standards.

'Mustn't sound smug,' she said, 'but I don't think of any as real failures. Of course, some have sold much better than others, but that isn't the test as far as I'm concerned. It tells what people wanted to read at the time, but not much about the quality. I've always been fortunate in discovering quite good titles. I would take a lot of trouble and spend time getting what I wanted. A good title is important and draws the reader. Take *Beyond Euphrates*. It says precisely what the book is about and where it is set. One of my most favourite of all is *The Southern Gates of Arabia*.' She smacked the back of one hand in self-reprimand. 'Really, this must stop! Praising oneself for one's own work!'

'How did you usually get the inspiration for a book title?'

'Actually, there's no formula and no pattern that I'm aware of. . . . It comes from being very close to the subject and trying to fix in your mind what the journeys, then the book, have been about. You don't want a long, rambling title: in any case, the publishers probably wouldn't have it! And, as I say, you want something that attracts readers who haven't themselves travelled there; or, if they have, would easily recognise it from the phrase. One of my last books is called *The Minaret of Djam*, as you know. All right, it's about Afghanistan and much more than a plain history of the minaret itself. But the journey to find the minaret became an objective, and so the minaret symbolises the country and everything I had gone there to do. . . .'

'Some of your titles are precise, such as *Rome on the Euphrates* or *Seen in the Hadhramaut* . . . quite lean and spare . . . others less so: *Dust in the Lion's Paw* and *A Peak in Darien*. Again, presumably the subjects have some bearing on them.'

'Yes, I think they have. In the case of the Roman history and the Arabian photographs, you know immediately what you're going to find when you open the book. The autobiography and the collections of essays are less easily determined and here again, like *The Minaret*, I seem to have looked for a symbol rather than an exact description of contents. *Perseus in the Wind* was probably derived the same way. It's also a favourite – well, at least at the moment!'

'Somebody writing about Herodotus said that he set the trend and indeed a standard for all travel-writers since his time: that he provided easy companionship for the road, took a close interest in surroundings and people, and found enough of the marvellous – even the unbelievably fantastic – to give his work stimulus and colour. He'd write about it all, occasionally tongue in cheek, but sympathetically and without too much censure. . . .'

'Oh, yes, and of course he *was* really the first. I think these attitudes apply equally well today. There's nothing more tedious than a writer who continually makes judgements upon behaviour as though his own beliefs were all that mattered. Conversely, a journey or an historical work without personality or bias is a rather weak, diluted affair and hardly worth reading. . . . The idea of offering companionship rather than education is important, however; since any education of readers will result from the work they are left to do by the author. The book then becomes a sort of partnership and the reader benefits in consequence. It's much more agreeable being pointed in the right direction than having information rammed down one's throat! Back again to my dear old godfather: that was the secret of his success as a lecturer, no question about it.'

'But surely some guidance is necessary also, over and above being merely shown the way?'

'The great thing lies in not overdoing it. The work of a writer is also concerned with entertainment. People should enjoy what they find in books. Apart from all that, however, it would be a monstrous conceit to imagine that you as writer are *capable* of giving the last word on a subject. In the end, if the reader has to use his wits, he'll be more appreciative than if you attempt to spoon-feed him, which is boring.'

'Your books, besides being filled with picturesque imagery, have also a strong historical bias. History, you've frequently admitted, has absorbed you since you were little; in fact, at one stage you studied history at Bedford College with the idea of taking a degree. And yet, when we were talking about this not long ago, you denied flatly my suggestion that you are, in part, a historian.'

'Well, if I did, it's quite simply because I am not; I'm what I'd describe as a lover of history. I don't have either the training or the professional insight of true historians, like Toynbee or Bryant. Seeing connections with the past and tracing them, I find thrilling; but that's really as far as it goes.'

'But you've written a very substantial history of *Rome on the Euphrates* which goes some way to supporting my suggestion.'

Freya grew animated in her anxiety to fend off the tag, which she appeared to find almost offensive: 'Oh, no! No! I would *never* agree to that! The *Rome* book gave me a lot of trouble. Such an enormous subject, so many lines to draw together. Really desperately hard work. It took me three years to finish; and one paragraph alone took a whole fortnight to get right! I have to admit, frankly, I was glad when the book was done. Three years is a long time.'

She felt particularly satisfied with the difficult paragraph when it had been completed.

'It's possibly the finest thing I've ever made. Now, that may sound immodest, but at my great age – and for some years past – I believe I've been able to judge whether a bit of writing is good or bad. The paragraph is an extended metaphor, an exceptionally difficult form. After I'd been up and down during the night scribbling notes here and there, and spending day after day revising and correcting it, I said to myself: "Better keep well away from complicated metaphors for a while, otherwise this book will never get written!" It was travelling down the Euphrates that first made me think of its ancient history and the part Rome had played. A true historian, like Professor Toynbee, would have approached the subject from quite a different direction, no doubt. I feel sure that he would have dug far deeper than I did – or, come to that, knew how to. His entire attitude of mind would have been different from mine . . . have encompassed an infinitely bigger view . . . been more relentlessly questing. A trained historian who has flair would have marshalled evidences and handled them with academic firmness; his work would have had the objectivity that the trained intellect eventually possesses. . . .'

I interrupted. 'Aren't you being just a trifle hard on yourself?'

'Perhaps . . . perhaps not. But I do want you to be clear where I stand in all this. It's true, my travel books all contain fragments of history; but then, so do most travel books. These aren't nearly enough to qualify me for the title of historian, even in an amateur sense. No, the correct discription must remain: a lover of history.'

'I would like you to read me the troublesome paragraph from *Rome on the Euphrates*. I've got it here beside me.'

'Of course, I'd be glad to read it.' I reached over and pulled the squat volume out of a shelf and handed it to Freya. She took a pair of spectacles from her bag and settled them on her nose.

She opened the book at about the middle, on her lap, and bent over it, turning page after page very slowly until she found the notorious paragraph.

'It's curious looking at one's work after so long. Makes one wonder why it should have been so hard to manage. The idea it attempts to express is important, however. From the writing point of view difficulty came in sustaining such a lengthy metaphor without overdoing it, or destroying the sense.'

She began to read in a firm, clear voice with increasing feeling, as if, in her thoughts, she recognised and embraced each phrase like an old friend.

' "The Aegean sea shows no horizon before the summer dawn. The morning breeze has not yet come to step between the islands; and in that enchanted hour day lies as if with closed eyes, iridescent as pearl and still involved with night. When the sun springs up with his spiked rays sea and sky separate, the horizon takes on its cutting-edge of sapphire, and the colour of the day is born. And sometimes, under the fulness of light as it progresses, a wide and gentle wave with no apparent wind to urge it heaves across the hollow spaces. The shocks that conceived it are forgotten as it whispers by without an obstacle in sight, and carries on its back a universe of wavelets and fluid shadows; and moves to shores that must break it. In the heyday and beauty of its power, during three brief generations, the 'eternity of the Roman Empire' moved thus across the world." '

She closed the book, took off her spectacles and dropped them into the little Kurdish handbag. Almost offhandedly, she said, 'Well, that's it.' She peered at her wristwatch. 'Half-past twelve . . . come along, you must be hungry.'

After lunch, Freya dozed for an hour, while I strolled leisurely up the Via Colmarin to the Rocca, then back down through the main square to the tower, where I found her playing Patience. She gathered up the cards with a little shrug: 'Not working out as it should . . . doesn't matter. Please, just remind me. We were saying something about dear Lawrence Durrell during lunch. Do you know him?'

'No, but I admire his books. I've also read a few of his novels and some poetry.'

'Such a pity we haven't seen each other for some time. I expect he's travelling . . . Egypt, somewhere like that. I think he still lives quite close to Nîmes . . . in winter they burn thorn-wood in their fires; reminds me of Roncevalles in the Pyrénées – you know, *ronce*, a thorn . . .'

For a few moments, she drifted into a world of distant recollections, far from Asolo and the tower.

She went on: 'I knew Lawrence when he lived in Cyprus. He was building a house, I think. He didn't have much money in those days. . . . Now, of course, he makes a good living from his books, which he deserves. He's a terribly nice man, although he did tend to run through wives! I don't know why that was. I told him once: "Lawrence, you can't treat a woman as a cat treats a tree, sharpening his claws on it all the time!" I think that took him back rather!' She laughed, fingering the big silver Euphrates ring on her right hand. 'He wrote a very flattering introduction to *The Journey's Echo* . . . he's really very kind; has a great talent. . . .'

I reminded her of some of Durrell's remarks: 'He praises your "poetic density"; says your work is "full of echoes"; good things like that.'

'As I say, very flattering and kind. I love some of his stuff: the four Egyptian novels; also *Prospero's Cell*, *Bitter Lemons*, and the other one about a Marine Venus. His descriptions of the sea-shore and Alexandria are lovely. I don't read fiction nowadays – actually I never have, apart from Meredith and Thackeray, and some Scott when I was young. Terrific descriptions of jousting and knights' dress and the whole medieval pageant. . . . All that's quite out of fashion I suppose. What was the name of Scott's great romance? *Ivanhoe*! That was a great excitement when I was a girl.

'Coming back to Lawrence Durrell, however: he's really a poet, and feels and sees like one. He shouldn't really call me a poet, however. But I don't really care for what I call his improper writings: the novels with Latin names. These reveal a side of Lawrence that I never saw.'

'Nevertheless, I'm sure you wouldn't allow disapproval of some of Durrell's work to interfere with an old friendship.'

'Oh, certainly not! It's only that I don't like these improper writings. I don't understand them and I dislike the characters. I'd never want to meet these people, who are so throughly disagreeable. Pity, don't you think, to write about such unpleasant subjects, when you can choose others so much more agreeable?'

'On the other hand, life is itself a rather inconvenient

mixture of good and bad. At the risk of sounding sententious, I believe novelists and poets should try to deal with life as a whole – good and bad together. You can't separate them in reality, so why do so in literature?'

'Yes . . . yes, I suppose so.' I could see that Freya had no intention of giving in. 'Doesn't help me to like the improper writings any better, however. After all, no one forces you to immerse yourself in the evil or unpleasant sides of life. They exist undoubtedly. We each have our dark aspect, that I don't deny for a minute. But surely there are ways of writing about it: ways of dealing with it in art.'

'I'm not quite clear what you're getting at.'

She half closed her eyes. 'I wish I could explain this better . . . find a ready example of what I mean. It isn't merely a question of technique. Literature has various laws which it pays one to follow; there are aspects such as construction which can be imparted to an extent. However, the creative side is in the hands of the individual writer. This can't be taught with a book of rules, like spelling or arithmetic. What I'm saying is, in order to write about the dark side of human character, we must find a creative method or solution. This in turn will vary according to the author . . . you see, it isn't essential to treat disagreeable themes disagreeably . . . maybe that's it.'

'I imagine experience has a big part to play in one's handling of difficult material. You go through all the processes of trial and error and discover what works, what doesn't work. Yet, somehow, it's never anything but hard grind. . . .'

'You know,' she replied, 'after all these years you would think that I, for instance, might have come to find writing easier to do. But, believe me, I haven't. It's just as difficult as it ever was!'

'Why do you think that is so?'

'Part of it is the business of seeing: as you achieve a certain mastery of your profession, so your standards rise. What would have passed years before with flying colours won't do any longer. Tricky . . . so much is to do with each artist's ability to gauge and perceive. I think that does come with experience, provided always that the experience is worth something and isn't just a matter of hammering away for a lifetime on one note! Then there's another question: do you think like a writer?'

'Which is evidently not the same as, let's say, a painter or a musician. . . .'

'No, I don't believe it is. Literature gives us an opportunity to make connections through time and space in a way that painting doesn't. I noticed the other effect very much when I was with my parents. They looked at things as if they'd been about to paint them. They'd look at a vase of flowers and see the shapes and colours, textures, light and shade and so forth. . . . I'd think about the flowers bursting from seed and blossoming and dying; I'd wonder about the life of the man who'd turned the vase on his wheel; perhaps try to picture the country where its clay was found. . . . We would all enjoy the flowers and smell their scent, but we'd each see quite different things. I suppose words are, to me, what colours were to my father and mother. And besides, literature has many other peculiarities.' She burst into sudden laughter. 'I suppose I must be one of them! That's one advantage of being old, you see; you can do pretty much what you like and nobody minds. . . . In fact, they even think it's quite all right!'

'Asolo seems to have served its painters and sculptors better than its writers from the point of view of companionship. I reckon artists of your parents' generation had a jolly sort of life, painting during the day and discussing art in the evenings at supper. You, however, don't have many other writers to talk to.'

'I know . . . it's rather a shame. There are one or two: my neighbour, Shirley Guiton, whom you know, writes with great sensitivity about the Lagoon. Let's see, who else? Oh yes, Cino Boccazzi: he's written a biography of Lawrence. Spends a lot of time searching for lost cities and vanished civilisations in Africa. His study at Treviso is filled with the bones of dinosaurs and all sorts of prehistoric creatures. . . . Dear Cino used to practise medicine: must have been alarming for the poor patients, having all those bones lying about. . . .'

'Well, if there aren't many writers to talk to, what do you like doing best when there's nobody staying and you've got the evenings to yourself?'

'Oh, I listen to the news on the wireless and have my dinner and I also read a lot. I'm very happy really to sit there with one of my Greek or Roman authors. Then I hear the second lot of news at a quarter to nine and after that I usually go to bed and read until I'm tired. Sometimes I wake up and read during the night as well.'

'I remember you telling me once that you were never bored.'

Freya nodded eagerly. 'Well, that's true, you know. It doesn't bother me in the least if I sit for days on end at the flat with just books and the wireless. My maid comes in twice a day and prepares breakfast and dinner, takes care of the laundry and shopping and tidies up. I'm really very fortunate in this respect, for having to cope with housework and cooking every day would drive me to distraction. Thank goodness, I'm spared all that! As you see for yourself, whenever you come down, the one tiresome labour that never lessens is replying to dozens and dozens of letters. I dread going away even for a few days to Switzerland or England. By the time I get home again, there's a heap waiting, like this.' She raised her hand high above her lap.

'Mind you, you're in a way responsible for this, for you write a lot of letters yourself. Do you remember, we worked out the other day that you'd written on average more than a letter a day, every day, for the past fifty years?'

'As many as that? Of course, when I was travelling in the

Middle East, I found it much more convenient to sit down beside a stream and scribble a letter to my mother or a friend than keeping a diary. People at home were kept in touch and didn't have to worry about me; and I could send off a little packet or two and avoid having to carry a diary which might, in any case, get lost. Then when I came to write my books, there they all were. Amazing how little scraps of detail are kept fresh in letters; much fresher than we generally manage in books.'

'There was a review of your latest collection of *Letters* in which they were criticised for being too polished and evidently written with a view to publication. That must have annoyed you.'

Freya smiled: 'Actually, it did. . . . I thought, "I'm not going to lie down under that!" And so I wrote to the reviewer, who was a very nice man from Ireland, and explained that my letters had mostly been written at the roadside while my men were setting up the camp or cooking our supper. I told him the great changes that have taken place in language during the past half-century probably account for what was written spontaneously fifty or sixty years ago seeming like the result of conscious effort today. Literature, as I keep saying, is in a bad way just now: so much rubbish being written for money or advertisement, with no real thought, much less affection, for language. Anyhow, the man wrote me a nice letter back, telling me he agreed!'

'Nobody could accuse you of compromise, where your work has been concerned. When you believe in something, you really do stick to it, do or die!'

'No sense in being obstinate for the sake of it; but where good taste is involved and belief in one's art, that's another affair. I've known many first-rate writers in my life: men like Bernard Berenson, David Cecil, Sidney Cockerell. . . . They would agree, or have agreed, that you don't compromise where standards are concerned. Dear old B.B. had always something remarkable to say – he was a true original: I remember being with him among some ruins which he specially loved, hearing him order his lunch to be sent up to where he was, because he couldn't bear to be parted from them. Great travellers of that period often wrote splendidly. Aurel Stein, for instance. Do you know *On Ancient Central-Asian Tracks* by any chance?'

She halted, poised in recollection. 'I met him once on a mountainside in Asia . . .' It sounded as if it might as easily have been Piccadilly. 'He came out of his tent and we talked for half an hour. His entire conversation was about how much he loathed and detested women travellers! In the end, I said that I supposed I ought to apologise for being alive at all; but we parted good friends and I was glad to have met him and told him so.'

The anecdote about Sir Aurel Stein jogged my memory. 'Do you think that there's been any special advantage or for that matter disadvantage in being a woman in the two worlds you inhabit principally – literature and travel?'

'No, I don't think so. Not everybody agrees all the time with what one writes and of course the Arabists' world has always been fiercely competitive. I daresay some of them don't think either my travels, such as they've been, or my books, amount to much. Well, that's up to them. Being a woman has saved my life, at least once, when I went into districts in Persia where a man would have been shot straight away. I let strands of my hair down under my hat and my guide shouted out to the tribesmen we met that I was just a traveller interested in their country; and so they let me go on. Venetia Buddicom and I found exactly the same reaction when we visited the Jebel Druze in nineteen-whenever-it-was . . . nobody paid any heed to a woman. Sobering thought, isn't it?'

'A lot of people seem to think that, in general, you prefer men's company to women's. Could this be because your profession as a writer and your predilections as a traveller have taken you into what was hitherto a male preserve?'

'I judge the matter of company, like most other things, on its merits. I'd far rather talk to an interesting woman than a boring man any day! Sex doesn't come into this. In fact, I've been drawn all my life by abstract, rather than concrete, episodic themes and I've found among my friends that very often men, rather than women, find such things interesting. I'm also interested in politics; here again, in the past, I found that men, rather than women, tended to discuss them. In a curious way, the fact that I've never been what one might term a great beauty has been an advantage, since the men I've known have spoken their minds freely without distractions, and their wives haven't needed to feel jealous!'

'It's very flattering to remember how people have confided in one. The result was that I very often saw a side of great soldiers or historians which wasn't generally known. Lord Wavell, whom I was very fond of, is a good example. Almost all the biographies of Wavell stress the military career and leave you knowing very little about the man as a whole. He and I used to talk about literature and all sorts of unmilitary subjects, when I stayed with them in India. He told me that his little collection, *Other Men's Flowers*, didn't represent favourites of his own, necessarily; but rather snatches of writing which he'd managed to read in the rare moments of relaxation when he could forget about the war. War was important to him, nevertheless; and he once told his son, Archie John, who was later killed by Mau Mau in Kenya, that, to be successful, a soldier must love war. Poor Archie John: I don't think he did. . . .'

'I noticed a biography of Lord Wavell, called *The Chief*, in one of the shelves. Is it a good one?'

'Yes, that's one of the best I've read,' she answered. 'But I do think it unfortunate that always the stress is laid on the soldier rather than on other aspects. It's quite reasonable that it should be so . . . yet, it leaves me dissatisfied.'

The question of the Wavell biographies was left unresolved. For a while we sat together, talking about books and journeys, Freya facing out towards the plain, Shelley's Hills as she called them, and the Lagoon; I facing the Alps, or, to be more accurate, a faded blue haze where the Alps should have been. The yellow afternoon sunshine warmed the room and slowly curled the thin cover of a paperback lying on the oval table. The book caught Freya's attention.

'What volume is that?' she inquired. 'Is it one of yours?'

'Not exactly. It's a life of the explorer, Burckhardt. We gave it to you last summer, in London.'

'Then what do you suppose it's doing up here?' She looked puzzled. 'It should be among the other travel books down at the flat.' She paused and bit her lip. 'You know, it's too dreadful! I remember now, I brought it with me to lend to *you*! My memory is shocking. All the facts are there, but the delivery service isn't what it used to be. Did I tell you, I was dining in someone's house recently, talking to a nice man sitting next to me; I looked closely at him and said, "You know, it's strange, but I'm certain that we've met somewhere before tonight." He replied: "I jolly well think we have; we've known each other for nearly fifty years!" To make matters worse, he was my host! Unforgivable, not recognising the person whose dinner-party it was. . . .'

After a moment or two of silence, I said: 'I could quite happily spend six months or a year among your travel books, reading them one by one. It's a marvellous collection.'

Freya looked pleased. 'Yes, it isn't too bad; mind you, they've been slowly accumulating for an awfully long time. At least now I've succeeded in establishing some order; unlike the poor scattered collections here in the tower.'

The travel books were kept at her flat in shelves that lined one entire wall of a corridor off the hall, leading to a guest bedroom. Starting from the bedroom end, the books followed the chronology of Freya's own travels: that is, Iraq, Persia, Southern Arabia, Turkey and so on, with a small shelf or two of African journeys wedged in above Iraq. Freya had visited Kenya, Tanzania and Uganda in 1959, but East Africa was not one of her main interests. The two bottom shelves, or rather sequences of shelves, running the length of the corridor, contained selections of photographs taken on expeditions over a period of forty years, from 1928. They were arranged in fifty-six landscape albums with green or beige matching covers and linen spines.

On the opposite wall, a low glass-fronted bookcase held volumes on mountaineering and the Dolomite valleys; military history; literary biography; and collected essays by W.P. Ker, as well as Ker's standard works on *The Dark Ages* and *Epic and Romance*. The wall above the bookcase was lined with pastel sketches of Asolo by Robert Stark.

'When you go to the travel collection nowadays, which areas do you find attract you most? Or which authors writing about areas of special interest to you. . . .'

Her expression became thoughtful. 'In a sense, you're talking here about two different things: countries which interest me and where I've travelled; and writers. As far as countries themselves go: well, of course Arabia never fails to excite me. My Hadhramaut journeys were, for me, a wonderful experience. In a small way, I was able to see and share some of the life of people whose ancient traditions are disappearing. Arabia has always had this effect of exciting European travellers in a way that few other countries can. They would go there; be – as they say – "bitten" by the desert and the nomad tribes; go back to Europe always longing to return. The magnetic pull of Arabia is mysterious and a kind of enchantment. . . .'

She rearranged the folds of her skirt and settled into a more comfortable position.

'I go to the shelves and take down Burton, or Doughty, or Philby and immediately I find myself back in their world: the gravel plains and the camels and the little tents where we camped at nightfall, where I would sit with a lamp and do my embroidery under the stars. There's an immense gulf between Doughty and Burton, of course, from the point of view of *how* they travelled. Burton, when he visited Medina and Mecca, went in disguise: in fact, it's unlikely that he could have done his journeys otherwise. Doughty found the idea of disguise unbearable and declared himself to the mob as a Christian, a *Nasrani*. Doughty was the true essence of the Englishman, proud of his Anglo-Saxon stock, whereas Burton was happiest when skulking unsuspected and unrecognised in an alley, listening to gossip and risking his neck.'

'I've been thinking about Viva Jeyes giving you Doughty's book in 1924 and its effect upon your whole life and career. Yet, bearing in mind that what it did was to open your eyes to the Arab world, it seems to me that the result might have been the same if instead she had given you Burton's *Pilgrimage to Medinah and Mecca* or Cheesman's book about the Empty Quarter.'

Freya regarded me critically. 'That's just the point: it wouldn't have been the same at all! I'm interested in Burton's observations; he's a vivid writer and a virtuoso. He plunges into every aspect of Arab life: masters the language; learns how to wear the clothes and move about like an Arab; studies their religion. But he's like a chameleon. Ready to change his colours to suit whatever background he happens to be involved with. Doughty's risk, travelling as an unbeliever among fanatical tribes was, I think, far greater than Burton's ever was. Also Doughty's absorption with geology and the stories told by layers of rock – like leaves of a book being parted after centuries – and his dedication to the English language, literature and poetry; all these gave Doughty a special fascination.'

'You read *Travels in Arabia Deserta* almost exactly a year after W.P. had died. Perhaps you found in Doughty a kind of Arabist equivalent for your godfather. . . .'

'I've never actually put those two events together to make a conclusion,' she said. 'Might easily be something in what you suggest, however. There *are* great similarities. Both men of action; both scholars; both lovers of literature and especially the English literary tradition. You also mentioned writers on the Empty Quarter, I think Cheesman?'

'That's only because the other books that come to mind, by Thomas and Philby, were written in the 1930s: Cheesman's was published in 1926, before you went to study Arabic in Lebanon.'

'Ah yes. . . . I see what you mean. In any case, reading about the Empty Quarter, however interesting that might have been, wouldn't have got me involved with the Arabs as Doughty did. People, history, ancient lines of tradition and activity coming down through time – these drew me. The empty desert wastes where few men had gone, Bedouin included, never attracted me. I've done a certain amount of exploration, in Persia and in Arabia' – she chuckled – 'even been given those medals for it; but I wouldn't have wanted to go off into a totally barren country merely to be the first across, even assuming I could have matched the physical hardship.'

I asked how the travel collection had been put together. 'In general, did you collect books about a country in order to study it before you travelled there; or were you first of all excited by an area and afterwards began to collect whatever had been written by other travellers?'

Freya replied that, as one might expect, there had been a little of each. 'As I've said earlier, I used to read a good deal about a country before going there. . . . Not, as a rule, while I was actually travelling about. And then later on I'd find books about it that I hadn't read and, if I could afford to, I'd buy them.'

'By the time you'd bought the source-books and studied languages and made other arrangements, the preparation time for the early longer expeditions must have been considerable.'

'Oh, indeed . . . usually two years. There were skills to be learned, such as mapping for example.'

'Where and how did you first learn about that?' I asked.

'It's surely a very specialised job?'

'The Royal Geographical Society, as we both know, has always been marvellously helpful to travellers. When I wanted to learn, I went there and talked to a charming old man who had a room at the top of their house in Kensington. He gave me all the instruction I needed and then he took me into the park opposite – Kensington Gardens – and there we put his lessons into practice. I think the technique is known as triangulation. You work on little strips of paper, fixing each new point of landscape from others whose exact location you already know. I'm sure I would never be able to manage it now; but in the '30s it was all right and I was even able to map a forest area north of Teheran for the government, where no maps had previously existed. They gave me a gold watch as a present for having done it, which I wore for twenty years.'

'Photography was another early interest of yours.'

'That's right, it was. I don't remember how that came about. My family was always taking pictures and sticking them into family albums; and, of course, dear Herbert Young had been a keen photographer for years. In 1933 we bought the little camera, the Leica, I have now and still use it! It was number fifteen of that type and I'm told it's now a very valuable collector's piece. Anyhow, I quickly learned how to develop the films and did all that in my tent; but it was essential to get up at four in the morning – at any rate before dawn – to develop the negatives while the air and the little dishes of fluid were still cool. I got quite interested in photography and I calculated once that fully one quarter of the time given to travelling had been devoted to it. But, you know, rather like the letters I wrote home, it didn't occur to me then that my photographs would be published. I'm talking about the very early days. I just took what subjects interested me and never thought beyond that.'

'I like the little pencil and pen-and-ink sketches you made on some of your journeys: like those in the Hakkiari country, in Eastern Turkey. Still, perhaps photographs have been

A sketch of the Via Browning, Asolo, 1958, by Freya Stark

Freya Stark and Alexander Maitland in the tower garden, 1981
(*photograph by Margaret Maitland*)

Casa Freia, Asolo (*drawing by Alexander Maitland*)

Freya Stark back in her hammock, 1952

In Casa Freia, 1963

From Montoria, 1966 (*drawing by Freya Stark*)

more useful.'

'Perhaps. . . . I wish often that I had really learned how to draw and paint well. In spite of what my parents had to say, I think there was a tiny grain of ability there, which might have been given a life. My sketches really aren't up to much, although it's always nice when somebody says they like them. But from the viewpoint of recording these vanished worlds efficiently, I think I've done better sticking to photography.'

'The collection we're making of your photographs will be, if I'm right, the third. It would interest me to know what importance you attach to these collections, compared to the dozen or so travel-books you've written.'

'Oh, goodness, that's very difficult.' Freya cast about for inspiration. 'It's back to this business of the visual and the literary, isn't it? It may be, if my work has any lasting value, that people will judge each branch on its own merits. The pictures give impressions and the physical detail of worlds which time and progress have eroded away; there must be some importance in having records of these; in fact, the more records, the better. As well as giving the bare facts, the books, I hope, reveal these worlds through the eyes of an individual. It's a distilling process. As I said before, no two writers who have travelled through the same country will give quite the same portrayal. It would be pleasant to think that my little heap of material might be added to other heaps and that, together, a vision of these Eastern worlds can be recreated truthfully. After all, whatever one's own tastes, it's far better having twenty or thirty nineteenth-century authors on the shelves instead of just one or two: that way you get a wider view and that, in turn, helps you to get closer to what *their* period was like.'

'Travel-books tend to have somewhat repetitive titles, don't they? But maybe that's not so very surprising. Each person, after all, has either ridden an animal of some sort or walked or used a vehicle. Everbody looks at the new country and gets his or her impressions. We find Sir Aurel Stein pursuing *Alexander's Track* in the Indus valley; then you yourself following *Alexander's Paths*. You've described the life *Beyond Euphrates*; a few shelves away I find Douglas Carruthers's adventures hunting and travelling *Beyond the Caspian*. Think of the Arabian travellers: *Arabia Deserta, Arabia Felix, Arabian Adventure, Arabian Sands*.'

She agreed at once. 'I don't think, however, that we attach much significance to that. It's a question of telling readers what the book is about, where it's set – perhaps even a hint of what the author has been doing there. For instance, when somebody picks up my little narrative of *Riding to the Tigris*, he has a picture straight away of me going off on horses or mules to a great river in the Eastern Mediterranean. If the reader also has some sense of history, such a title would give him clues as to why I had been there and therefore what the book is liable to be about.'

'*Riding to the Tigris* is probably my favourite of all your travel books. In a way, besides being one of the shortest, it's also the purest.'

'When you say, the purest, what exactly have you in mind?'

'Just that it's a pure, narrative form. Unlike earlier works, you don't interweave narrative with letters; I'm not making comparisons, at least not deliberately, but I am saying that the straightforward narrative has a particular enchantment. Same again in *The Minaret of Djam*; but I like the Tigris book better.'

'This is very interesting: I was saying today how much I like *Perseus in the Wind*, that is, as far as one likes or dislikes anything one has written or made oneself. Yet, had we been talking then about travel-books, and you'd asked me, I would also have said I like *Riding to the Tigris*. The old books, written before the last war, *Valleys of the Assassins* and *A Winter in Arabia*, hold a special charm for me, since they describe my first experience of these countries. I was getting to grips with writing then, and, of course, I was forty-five years younger. All these make a difference to the viewpoint. As you say, it's only a hundred pages, but the essence of the journey is there; and probably better handled or evoked, or whatever one says, than in some of the other works.'

'It's also noticeable that, whereas, for instance, Burton's travel-writing ranged over a wide field, including South America, West Africa and India as well as Arabia, like Gertrude Bell you've restricted your writing to one main theatre – the Eastern Mediterranean. I'm referring obviously to your travel works rather than autobiography and don't count exceptions such as *The Minaret*, set in Afghanistan. . . .'

'Well, as you're aware, the Eastern Mediterranean has been my focus since the beginning. There's some advantage also to be gained from keeping to one's own little bit of territory. You're gradually associated with it; as you extend your experience – write more about it, travel more and more in it – so I believe you find deeper insights and make pictures which have greater meaning. You can't really expect to achieve such results if you flutter from one place to another, like a butterfly. I'm sure that Burton's other books are excellent: but they cannot possibly reflect more than he himself was able to assimilate, as a result of relatively brief encounters. Of course, he was a brilliant linguist and that made an immense difference to the quantity and quality of information he was able to gather. . . .

'Actually, that's of the greatest importance. There's just no earthly good travelling seriously or for any length of time in a country where you can't speak the language. This may sound obvious, but it's absolutely vital. When I began in Arabia, I'd been studying Arabic fairly continuously for eight or nine years, much of that time either living or travelling in the Middle East. Yet it wasn't until I got to Cairo, during the Second World War, and began to attend daily discussion groups with Arab clergy at the university, that I really understood the language. In Cairo, I spoke Arabic for twelve hours each day, every day: that was ages after I'd begun taking my first lessons from the old monk at San Remo, going and coming with a packed lunch once a week by train. . . .'

'Might this explain why you've never felt any desire to write about your visits to China or Africa or Indonesia; or your most recent journeys by pony in Nepal?'

'Yes, that's definitely part of the reason. In China, I wasn't allowed to go very far by myself; and because I didn't speak Chinese, I couldn't have any conversation. Children kept coming up and staring at my eyes, since apparently blue eyes or grey-blue eyes are uncommon. Africa, like China, was very brief and I wasn't doing anything particular except looking at the country and the animals. Nepal is the same: I'm just trekking up into the Himalayan foothills, but I've never been there for much longer than three weeks at a time and these journeys don't fit into the same category as those in Turkey or the early expeditions to Luristan or the Hadhramaut. There's no language difficulty, by the way, in Nepal, where they speak English, as they do in most parts of India.'

'If you returned to the Middle East, I wonder whether you'd find inspiration in the changed environment. After all, you've always acknowledged change as a fundamental part of life.'

She coloured. 'Nothing would persuade me to visit little towns and villages like Abu Dhabi or Kuwait, which I knew in the days when Kuwait, for instance, had sandy streets and its old walls around it and when camel-caravans came and went to and from the depths of desert. Now these places are full of motor-cars and hotels and ghastly buildings of all sorts. The East I've loved is the East that's gone, or almost gone . . . washed away in the revenues from oil . . . I find all that unbearably sad.

'Changes have come too suddenly; and there's something very wrong when centuries of tradition can be swept aside to make way for the grafted-on technology of a totally alien culture, such as we have exported from the West. I've never for a moment suggested that it would be right to keep the Arab tribes in a state of mummified antiquity, however much this might appeal to English romantics who love the desert. But change must be assimilated gradually and in Arabia it hasn't and the results show in the wreckage of these exquisite little towns. Nothing would induce me to go back there and I certainly would never want to write about any of that!'

'At least you have happy memories of Arabia and the rest of the Middle East before these changes started happening. And what you've experienced is enshrined in the volumes of your travel library.'

She smiled, as her passion subsided: 'That's so. For that very reason, I'm more than ever anxious that when I die, these books will go to a university library where they'll be taken out and studied by young people who will never see the East as I did. That way, they'll be useful; be used as books ought to be. Not left to moulder in some institution's vault.'

9

Space, Time and Art

ROBERT STARK's pastel sketches of Asolo appeared to me to differ markedly from paintings by Freya's mother – in one respect more than others. Flora's pictures eulogised, and somehow embalmed, a world that no longer existed: a world of children dressed in smocks, button-boots and black stockings, of men in hard collars, Norfolk-jackets and gaiters. Her world had closer ties with the medieval landscapes of Asolo which she had used to decorate an immense, pillared wardrobe in Freya's bedroom, than with the closing decade of the nineteenth century. On the other hand, the character of Asolo portrayed by Robert had altered remarkably little between his day and the present, at any rate visually.

I pondered these questions and eventually remarked: 'Those moonlit pictures by your father might have been finished yesterday. His work, more than your mother's, feels contemporary; yet I wonder why? After all, he was far more of a romantic, while she was involved, here in Italy, in daily affairs and ran a business.'

Freya did not respond immediately; then she said, 'A point to remember, however: very few of Father's pictures have figures in them. I mean those pictures you see here. My mother's work consists largely of figure-composition. Old buildings and landscapes date perhaps less obviously than style of dress and activities which fix Mother's painting in its period.'

'That's true. The only figure-studies I've seen by your father are the pencil sketches which he did while out hunting on Dartmoor; you know, the ones in the little pocket-sketchbook we discovered a day or two ago. . . . There again, hunting-costume hasn't changed all that much during the past seventy-five years and so those drawings don't look dated either.'

Freya nodded. 'Mother and he were both good painters, so I wouldn't have thought a feeling of period mattered.'

'It's just that I'd been thinking about what we'd been saying about Jane Austen and the Brontë sisters and wondering whether a sense of timelessness in prose corresponds to timelessness in painting?'

'What a pity darling B.B. or my dear father isn't here. Berenson would have given an opinion straight away. . . . I'm not a painter and I imagine I think more in literary terms. . . . But I'd say the two divisions of art were affected in much the same way. When you look at a Botticelli or a Raphael, you're struck immediately by the perfection of it. It's a statement of sheer genius and the fact that the people are wearing togas or medieval robes doesn't matter. Its meaning and its expression don't become passé; any more than a river scene by Monet seems old-fashioned; or girls in a poppy-field. Whereas, mannered, recherché paintings by the Pre-Raphaelites, striking as they are, seem to me period pieces. The difference is, Botticelli and Monet both worked in the present and were innovators. . . .'

'Maybe that describes your parents' painting. Whether or not they were innovators, your father more than your mother worked in the present.'

Freya grinned. 'That's quite possible. Apart from landscape, his great love was drawing and making sculptures of animals, and of course that's one of the charms of Nature and of the animal kingdom. The cycles repeat; seasons come and go. Birds build their nests, hatch their young and fly off to spend the winter in warmer climates. Each day dawns as a fresh experience. Nature is contemporary, whereas we humans, having memories more developed, return to the past in dreams or imagination and repine for better days. Secret of remaining contemporary is to avoid repining. . . .'

'Nevertheless, it must give you great pleasure having so many beautiful reminders of your parents round the walls.'

'Oh, yes!' she exclaimed. 'Pictures are so lovely that even if they brought sad rather than happy associations to mind their own beauty would soon overcome them. Everything triggers some emotion or other. For instance, Mother's little painting of Vera and me walking with Father across Dartmoor reminds me of how happy we were as children living there. Mother, sitting there painting, saw, I expect, only bleakness all round; but the very same bleakness and windswept skies were the things that appealed most to Father and me. So, you see, my dear mother and I, looking at this picture years afterwards, would do so always receiving quite opposite responses.'

'Portraits, especially, strike me as a little uncanny. I feel this less through paintings or sculptures than films or photographs, however. In one sense, the portrait *is* you; in another sense, it has nothing to do with you whatever.'

'But surely the two identities, your own as a living person and the portrait's, are one and the same? I admit, one is a representation of the living subject seen through the artist's eyes . . . is that what troubles you?'

'Yes and no. Really, I was thinking that the face one recognises on film, or in a portrait of oneself painted, say, ten years ago, is not the same person who stands looking at his or her own likeness . . . biologically, the whole system has changed and is constantly changing. Experiences affect one . . . age, health . . . all these separate the living person from the portrait.'

Freya considered. 'While you were downstairs this morning, making tea, I glanced through my *Life History* album. Now, there I find photographs of myself from the age of two months right up until my seventieth birthday, at Maser. Obviously I'm impressed with the physical changes that have taken place; a little gloomy to see myself putting on weight and getting older. But, to me, it's the same person – not at all what you appear to see, a whole series of different people in the same outward appearance. . . .

'Even if it's right, that our body alters completely every so many years, in a chemical sense, spirit and personality go on. It would be awkward, in fact, if they didn't. That is where true identity lies. However, I firmly believe that the personality does not survive death, as the spirit does. I like to imagine our spirit joining the flood of spiritual matter. . . . But, to think that we should open a gate and find ourselves surrounded by our families and friends is just absurd. Pure nonsense! When we die, I think personality vanishes with the life spark; rather like switching off the electric light. Ask yourself sometime: where does the light you've extinguished actually go?'

'The question of time and whether we see it as something we ourselves move through, or something itself in movement, occurred to me also, looking at the T'ang horseman beside your writing-desk. The imaginative spark that fired the sculptor had nothing to do with time, as such. One saw the time-factor expressed only in the style and workmanship.'

'Yet, it has the same purity that the Botticelli possesses,' she said. 'You see this all through the ages . . . that's what distinguishes the finest work, touched by the passing wings of genius. It comes right off the treadmill; stands immortalised and apart from lesser creations which tarnish and decay. . . .'

She waved a hand towards the rooftops, little towers half hidden by cypresses and the misty plain: 'All things considered, however, I do think that painters and sculptors have had a pleasanter time of it than writers! All those painters who used to visit us here, or in England, were a rather carefree, happy lot, full of gossip of their art or of who had painted this or that in such-and-such an exhibition. They'd eat their lunch and vanish off with an easel for the rest of the day. Mother might play for them in the evening; otherwise they would sit round talking.'

'It sounds a good life.'

'Oh, it was. Some of our friends were really quite talented: Herbert Olivier, who painted me when I was thirty, in 1923; he painted Herbert Young, that portrait downstairs. I gave the one of me to the National Portrait Gallery last year.'

Herbert Young had, in turn, portrayed Robert Stark with the camera, Stark wearing smart oatmeal tweeds carrying a portable easel. The cumbersome device supporting the canvas was attached to a projecting framework three feet long, strapped to his waist and shoulders, rather like a cinema usherette's ice-cream tray. The easel stood upright at the outer edge, with a shallow box between it and the artist's stomach, holding paints and brushes. Painting at the turn of the century had called for a degree of physical strength and stamina!

Freya went on. 'Did I tell you about my efforts to study drawing in Paris? Well, in fact, they produced quite good results . . . but things that happened! It was after the last war. We drew mainly from nude models; and, for some reason, my class consisted of women. Anyhow, every now and then the girl we were drawing would have a little rest, put on a dressing-gown and wander among us, chatting and inspecting our efforts to reproduce her form.

'One day, however, they brought in a man to pose. We thought nothing of drawing him without his clothes, as it happened, just as long as he remained on the daïs. But then, he, too, decided to have a rest and came round and stood beside each one of us: very polite, but absolutely naked! It was very disturbing having the great creature at one's shoulder. . . . The drawing-master told him next time he'd better put something on before beginning his little tour!'

'Your father had a long apprenticeship, hadn't he?'

'Seven years,' she replied. 'Terribly long time. He studied in Paris with Julian and learned a lot about anatomy.'

'Your father's sketches of Pen Browning's model with a python draped round her shoulders always amuse me. The python has such a contented expression on its face!'

Freya shook with merriment. 'Poor old python! Of course, Pen Browning wasn't up to much as a sculptor. Some of his stuff was really awful. He worked for years on scenes based on the Garden of Eden . . . paid local peasant girls to pose for him. Then one day a fair came to Asolo, with all sorts of wild animals in cages and that's how Pen got the python; bought it from the fairground people. The python spent most of its life asleep, waking up only occasionally for a little food. Pen used to carry it everywhere in a wooden box. Once he took it to England and a customs-officer asked what the box contained. . . . Then insisted that Pen open it up. In spite of Pen's repeated warnings, the customs man had kept banging the sides of the box while he examined it. All this banging woke the python which had been sleeping peacefully inside. When they got the lid off the box, the python put its head outside to see what was going on, and cleared the customs-shed in a twinkling!'

Freya sighed: 'The poor python had a sad end! Pen had been making more sculptures of Eve in the Garden, with the python wound round the model's bare shoulders, rather like a stole. Suddenly, without warning, the python awoke . . . must have been spring stirring in its blood – or perhaps it was merely hungry – anyway, it began to squeeze the wretched girl and Pen had to shoot it with a pistol he kept in a drawer for just such an emergency!'

I said that I had never seen any of Pen Browning's work and remarked that it might be interesting, even if it were poor, because of connections with Asolo and the Brownings' poetry.

'Well, as I told you, Pen's sculpture was rather dreadful. As far as I remember, there used to be a good many in the

Town Hall. However, one day the mayor visited my mother and said they needed repairing and what did she advise? Mother went along with the mayor and had a look and then they got hammers and, between them, smashed up the whole lot! It sounds like terrible vandalism, but the sculptures were in very poor condition and not worth keeping; otherwise she'd certainly never have done it. . . .'

'Pen Browning, from your description, seems to have been a rich, rather unfulfilled dilettante. . . .'

'Yes, he was. Quite different altogether from my parents, who were amateurs, but very gifted, properly trained and so on.

'They were never short of money, except now and then after a little moment of extravagance. Neither had much sense where money is concerned, which, of course, comes of being artists. Still, we seemed to manage fairly well. At one time, I think we had five houses, scattered about . . . just imagine, five houses! Makes no sense at all. No wonder there was never enough time for painting! An artist should never get into circumstances where house or gardens or other affairs force his real work into second place. That's just no good at all. Artists must have freedom and tranquillity and solitude in order to do their work. These are vital to a serious artist.'

'Just now, you remarked that painters, in your opinion, had a better life than writers. You explained why you thought some of the social ingredients were preferable, but did you mean also the painter's *work* as opposed to the work of the writer?'

'Oh, most definitely! Painters go off to the studio or into the countryside and, at the end of a day or two they see a beautiful result. The poor writer sits alone at his table, wracking his brains for a few hundred words and after three or four hours gives up, totally exhausted. In the evening, he goes back and reads over what he's written and thinks, oh, what rubbish! and throws the lot into a basket.' She smiled. 'To be fair, I myself don't find writing quite as bad as that! I work

Freya Stark riding near Aleppo, 1958

Zab defile from Hakkiari, 1958 (*drawing by Freya Stark*)

Buildings at Side, 1961 (*drawing by Freya Stark*)

The Bosphorus, 1966 (*drawing by Freya Stark*)

Amorgos, 1966 (*drawing by Freya Stark*)

Anadolu Hisar, 1966 (*drawing by Freya Stark*)

Freya Stark, 1981 (*photograph by Piers Quirk*)

very slowly and take a long time finding the word or phrase I want. At the end of the day, I usually find I don't have to alter a great deal of what I've written.'

'I expect, like most writers, you find there's a time limit beyond which you cannot usefully go. I've often wondered whether such a limit applies equally to novelists as to biographers, travel-writers and historians? The work they're doing is to some extent different, after all.'

Freya said she was sure that it did. 'Whether you're writing a novel or a biography or re-living memories of a journey, it's all creative work you are involved in. I do appreciate the point you're making. . . . It's a matter of distinguishing between the inventive element in fiction and the work of recreating vanished personalities and landscapes. . . . Of course, these call for different skills; but the effect on the writer's ability to work for more than three or four hours at one go appears to be the same. I once asked Alan Moorehead how long he would spend each day writing and he told me, "Three to four hours is the most I'm able to do. After that, nothing good comes."'

Freya gazed out of the window. 'Look there! Look at the swallows circling over Pen Browning's little tower. . . . So very pretty it all is in the afternoon light.'

'Strange, isn't it – for all we've talked about your travels in such exotic places, we haven't mentioned birds or animals; well, except perhaps for horses . . . oh, and of course the python.'

'I'm sure I don't know why that should be,' she replied. 'I've no scientific, nor indeed any specialised knowledge of the animal world, but I've always loved them for what they are. Father taught me a lot about horses; and we always had a little dog at home. We called my dear father "Pips", after a little terrier we were very attached to and I had a sheep-dog here in Asolo until quite recently. He used to wander into the drawing-room . . . very quietly, just to see what was happening.

'Of all the animals I've had as pets, I think my favourite was Himyar. Years ago, when I was travelling in the Hadhramaut, I saw some boys throwing stones at something on the ground. It was a lizard and I knew that if they continued they'd kill it. I suppose they wanted to eat the poor little thing. I intervened. . . . The boys weren't at all happy that I had robbed them of their dinner, but the little lizard seemed to appreciate it! It reminds me, years later in Turkey I was nearly killed myself by boys throwing stones at me in one of the villages . . . big stones, the size of a teacup! Made me aware of what poor Himyar must have felt that day in South Arabia. . . .

'Anyhow, for a long time he wouldn't touch any food and I feared he would die of starvation. I used to put him on my lap with a leaf or two and stroke his head and try to encourage him. After about a month, he got over his feeling of strangeness and began to eat normally.'

'Why did you call him Himyar?'

'Oh, after the name of the tribe from which I had rescued him – the Beni Himyar. I carried him back here to Asolo and bought him a cage to sleep in at night; and during the day I'd take him for walks in the garden. . . . He had a lead and a little harness, just like a dog. He liked lettuce, but his favourite food was either violets or carnations, both of which I grew in the flower-beds. When I took him to London once, I used to buy a little bunch of violets for him every day for a shilling . . . poor man selling them would probably have been shocked to think of his lovely flowers being fed to an Arabian lizard!'

She smiled wistfully. 'I remember, too, what happened when the aeroplane from Venice flew over the garden. Himyar would press himself flat against the grass, as the shadow of the plane passed overhead. Wretched little creature! He thought the plane was some gigantic bird of prey . . . he was utterly petrified!'

There had been problems looking after Himyar when

Freya was travelling or staying with friends. It had been easy to start with; but, as he grew bigger and more conspicuous, so he was apt to make his presence felt. Freya recalled how the lizard had crawled out of the bosom of her coat in the crowded dining-car of a train and caused a general panic among the women passengers. Another time, in England, a friend's housekeeper left a curt note in Freya's bedroom, complaining that Himyar's claws scratched the furniture. But invariably, she grinned, owners of houses themselves – even their wives – came to appreciate Himyar after they had been properly introduced.

'What happened to Himyar in the end?'

'That was terribly sad; really all my fault. He had a little cage, with a cushion and a light. But I foolishly didn't realise that he would wish to hibernate and I think being deprived of hibernation killed him. I'd made no allowance . . . I was terribly upset. The little animal had such great character. When I came down to breakfast in the morning, he'd run up and down the bars of his little cage to greet me. I became really very fond of dear Himyar.'

There had been other pets, including the Siamese cat in the cover photograph of the collected *Letters*. However, Freya explained that her latest animal companion had been a Tibetan pony, named Rati-Gori, which means, Red Bells, which she had ridden up the Nepalese valleys on her two latest Himalayan expeditions. 'Red Bells, or as I call him, Ponie, is a wonderful creature,' she exclaimed. 'Without him, I would never have made these last journeys to the mountains. We reached together nearly as far as the Tibetan frontier. You should see some of these mountain tracks . . . no more than this wide!' She held her hands about eighteen inches apart.

'Pretty frightening, I can tell you! I tried always not to look down and kept my eyes in front or thought of the views which, from these hillsides, at twelve or thirteen thousand feet, were marvellous. Ponie's footing was absolutely sure, as you'd expect from an animal that's lived all its life among mountains. He had a rather bad habit, however, of walking right on the outer edge of the path, dislodging little stones with his hooves and sending them rattling hundreds of feet down! He wasn't shod, of course, but his hooves had got accustomed to the hard going. I would try my utmost to interest him in the side of the track nearer the mountain-face, but it was useless . . . always wandered to the dangerous side. . . . He reminded me of English friends who come here to stay in summer and take me out for drives. They begin always on the proper side for Italy, which is the right; but then, as we motor along, they start talking and the car drifts gradually farther to the left. To drive anywhere with them is like courting certain death! You know how Italians drive: no mercy shown to foreigners whatever!'

'The Sherpas presumably helped you to guide Ponie, at any rate where the going got very bad: I'm thinking of landslides, steep riverbanks. . . .'

'The Sherpas were all extremely kind,' she said, beaming. 'But on my last trip, there was one Sherpa, very nice really, who irritated me by holding on too much. Where the track had been washed away by a downpour, or where we had to cross one of those rope-bridges that swing about a lot, help was necessary. I explained that, elsewhere, I would prefer to manage with less attention – at the same time I tried hard not to offend him. It was difficult and required great diplomacy! When we approached the steepest hills, I used to stand upright in the stirrups, to help Ponie by keeping my weight off the saddle. It made a big strain on my legs, and I had his mane in my face all the time. Shows how severe these Himalayan inclines must have been! All this has been recorded on the film we made of my trek and you'll see that I'm not exaggerating. . . .'

She sat forward in her chair, patted her waist and held her arms akimbo. 'Nothing like Himalayan trekking for getting extra weight off . . . beats all those health-farms and so-called diets hollow! Last February, I lost eleven kilos. Perhaps that was a shade too much . . . this winter, I lost some more; can't remember offhand how many. It was all the work of standing in the stirrups, keeping my weight off Ponie's back. Strenuous, but I enjoyed every minute!'

10

Setting Forth

TWILIGHT slowly dimmed the room as we sat talking. Mist still obscured the mountains, except for a glimpse of a jagged ridge, suspended like a cloud above the roofs of Santa Anna monastery. We watched the daylight fade and the shadows deepen. Freya's Euphrates ring scribbled gleaming traces in the dusk.

'I thought you didn't wear the silver ring unless you were abroad?' I said.

'That's quite right,' she replied. 'Today, for some reason, I felt like wearing it, but it's really a talisman – a sort of desert St Christopher – and so I keep it, as a rule, for journeys.'

She slipped it off and handed it to me. 'Heavier than it looks, isn't it? Still, it has had a lot of work to do. An old man on the Euphrates gave it to me about 1935. He came from a tribe of silversmiths. You probably can't see very well in this light, but it's engraved with a lion, a scorpion and a mosquito; and they, in turn, are encircled by a snake. These are the desert creatures that might do a traveller harm; but the ring gives protection. . . .' She smiled: 'Touch wood, seems to work!'

I gave her back the ring: 'Shall I switch on one of the table-lamps? Or do you prefer the twilight?'

'I rather like sitting about in the dark. We might have just one lamp, however; perhaps the one on the writing-desk. That won't spoil the effect. Sitting in the shadows, like this, reminds me a little of the desert. . . . After the sun goes down, there's very little light except from your fire, if you have a fire, or perhaps a tiny oil-lamp. Not really sufficient to read by, or write letters. That's probably why Arabs and nomads of all sorts are such good conversationalists.'

'I suppose you go to bed early when you're travelling in remote places.'

'Not very early,' she answered. 'You know, half-past nine, ten o'clock, something like that. The Arabs love to talk, as I say, and they've made a real art of it. One man will begin and say his piece . . . takes his time over it and carries on until he's finished. Nobody interrupts him; interruption is considered the height of bad manners. What a change from the West, especially southern Europe, where conversation becomes a sort of battle with everybody talking at once, shouting, in order to get their little bit said. The Arabs go about all this in a far more civilised manner. Each person has plenty of time to speak. Everybody else listens. . . .'

'Suppose nobody wants to answer the speaker, or there's simply nothing more to add to the particular discussion, do Arabs fill in the gaps between with small-talk, as so often happens here. People find silences embarrassing, after all.'

'Here, they do seem to find that . . . but never in Arabia. If someone finishes his speech and nobody has a ready answer, they all sit round in perfect silence until another person wishes to speak; and then he goes on, and again nobody interrupts . . . so on and so on, like that. There's a good deal to commend it. For one thing, you have a chance to hear exactly what's being said and a chance to consider your reply.'

'It's a good many years since you travelled in the desert, isn't it? When you were showing me photographs of the black tents and pictures of your more modest expeditions through the Villes Mortes and some of the Turkish valleys, for example, I couldn't help wondering when the urge to travel would come again and where it would lead.'

'Always some little plan developing slowly,' Freya replied. 'But, really, I haven't done too badly during the past year or eighteen months. I've been twice to Nepal; once purely as a traveller, second time with the film people – dear Colin Luke and his Indian photographers. Where else? Ah, yes, Turkey and Syria . . . Indonesia; and of course my usual little trips to England and Switzerland. Now, considering everything, including the fact that I'll be ninety next birthday, I can scarcely complain of being stuck in Asolo.'

'Asolo, now that you mention it, is beautiful, really idyllic; but I do see how it might become claustrophobic and make you feel quite desperate to get away.'

'I love Asolo . . . lived here, off and on, for the best part of a century, after all. I feel a great security in the old walls . . . that's a feeling I never had when I lived out in the hills at Montoria. Montoria was sheer perfection: the lovely sloping gardens which Lanning Roper helped me make . . . wonderful views of the hills and a great vista of the plain, right out as far as the Lagoon. You could see the water of the Lagoon sparkling in the sunshine on a clear day – well over fifty kilometres away. But I was twice visited by gangs of people after dark and I decided then that it was time to move.'

'What happened exactly?'

Freya appeared to concentrate her thoughts on the Euphrates ring, twisting it round and round her finger as she spoke. One night, she said, about twelve o'clock, after she and her old housekeeper had gone to bed, a party of five young men arrived, demanding to be let in. Standing at the head of the steps armed with a revolver, Freya confronted them. After a brief discussion, one of the intruders inquired, 'Signora, have you any bullets in your little toy?'

Freya replied, 'Five, the same number as yourselves.' At that point, the men departed. . . .

As she explained, the second visit was more alarming.

'A big car drove up to the house in the middle of the night . . . full of people. I came out on to the balcony and stood in the moonlight, looking down at them. They told me they wanted to see over my house – that I must let them in at once.

My poor old housekeeper was indoors, terrified out of her wits. . . . I held up my revolver, so that they could see it clearly, and told them to go. They argued and argued . . . the whole thing was very unpleasant. Then they got into their car and started the engine. I simply couldn't resist and fired a shot above them . . . the car and occupants vanished like smoke! I had a warning siren installed by then and set it off, hoping to attract some attention . . . not a bit of it! Next morning various farmers and people who lived nearby came along and said, "We heard your siren last night. . . . Was anything the matter?" '

'What about the police?' I asked. 'Surely you telephoned for help. . . ?'

'Well, by then it was too late. I did speak to the police, but Montoria is seven or eight miles from Asolo and the nearest police-station; the police explained that they would have to put on their uniforms, since it was undignified to arrive wearing only pyjamas; and by the time they'd managed all that, the robbers – or whatever those people were – had got clean away. . . . At that stage, I felt it was time to return to Asolo . . . besides, the gardens at Montoria were steep and too big to manage easily; and my old housekeeper, who'd been with me for fourteen years, hated being marooned in the depths of the country. . . .'

'Now of course, from the travel point of view, you can come and go easily as often as you like. No gardens to attend to; no large house that needs constant looking after, locking up and so forth. Nevertheless, you must miss Montoria, just as you often say how much you missed Casa Freia, despite the inconvenience.'

'One can't have it all ways, however. Houses are fine, if you intend to live in them all the year round – or most of the year – have plenty of help . . . plenty of money for running expenses and repairs. But, at my age, a house is a dreadful tie. The flat down in the Via Canova, and the tower here in Caroly's garden, suit me ideally. The flat's close to the hotel, where I have lunch; there aren't too many stairs; and the tower is available if any friends want to come and stay. I need both, as a matter of fact, if only to store my furniture and books. Having lived for so long in large houses, I've accumulated quite a lot . . . things inherited, other things bought over the years. It would upset me very much to sell them, just in order to squeeze into some smaller space. However, now I can lock the flat and go where and when I please, for as long or as short a time as I like. I've an excellent maid, as you know, who sees to the flat, and dear Caroly watches over it and the tower until I get back. I don't think I've ever been quite so free in my life! It's really wonderful . . . a way of life I highly recommend!'

'Where do you think you might go next?'

'All this lamplight and shadow reminds me very much, as I say, of the tents and going about in Persia and Arabia. However, Arabia doesn't interest me any more – at least the places they've modernised don't – and I doubt that I'd manage the parts of Persia I used to know. I would like very much to go to the south, see southern Persia where there are ruined cities and where the landscape remains, I'm told, very much as it was. I still speak the language in a rusty sort of fashion; but in any case it would all come back when I'd got there and was actually travelling. Languages I find quite easy; I suppose because of starting so early.'

'I do envy people, like your godfather who could speak and write so many languages fluently . . . you told me W.P. had fifteen.'

'No point sitting about being envious: do something about it! Envy gets you nowhere!' Freya chuckled; but I realised that, underneath it all, she was serious. She went on: 'Altogether, I could speak about ten . . . don't think I can remember them quite so easily now. Let's see, what were they. . . ? Apart from the classical side – Greek and Latin – I had Italian, French, German; Arabic, Turkish, Persian; English of course, and a little Spanish, a smattering of Urdu, but oddly enough not *modern* Greek, despite the fact that I've spent so much time in the Aegean and wandering about the mainland of Greece.' She clicked her tongue: 'Oh, and I quite forgot to mention Russian which I learned from gramophone records. . . .'

'You make it all sound so easy, but surely one must have some flair for languages . . . it takes more than the desire to travel in a particular country. . . .'

'Nothing is easy if you don't apply yourself in the vital stages . . . it becomes easy only after you have a routine which helps you build up a vocabulary and get some understanding of grammar. There's no sense whatever trying to absorb more than you're able to, without making the work tedious. If you carry a little dictionary and learn the same number of new words every day, let's say a dozen, you keep going back to the dictionary and jotting down the spellings until you're sure of them . . . that way they're apt to stick in the memory. By the end of a week, you've learned almost a hundred . . . four hundred after a month. At that stage, you can make simple conversation, get about, mix with people and learn how the new language really works.'

'Just now you mentioned records. . . .'

Freya nodded enthusiastically. 'Yes. They're excellent. Far better than a book, because you hear the words being spoken and that helps enormously with pronunciation. The main thing with any new language is to speak it . . . writing can come later. For the traveller, speech is the important thing.'

'You shouldn't have any difficulty planning new journeys with such an impressive list of tongues at your disposal. If you want to visit Persia, for example, it wouldn't take very long, presumably, to brush up enough of the language to manage comfortably.'

'Oh, no, indeed . . . that would be a simple matter, assuming my wretched brain will consent to work and memory perform a little more efficiently than it has done lately! I would love to visit China, you know . . . not as I did twenty years ago, as a tourist pure and simple, but having acquired enough Chinese to travel independently about the country. Alas, I think it's too late for that now: brushing up a language I've spoken for years is one thing. Learning a completely new one is another affair. In any case, Chinese isn't related to any languages I already know and they don't use the Roman alphabet. All these little pictures would floor me completely. It's a shame, for I'd love to have visited some remote part of the country . . . perhaps Western China, with the forests and mountains and strange animals like the Giant Panda. Anyhow, that's just dreaming. . . .

'There is Nepal, of course. I would be very excited to go again and look at Kanchenjunga; then go to the Sherpa villages in Eastern Nepal and stay among the people there for a while. When I was there last year, the Sherpas invited me to come to their region. They're delightful, kind, considerate people and nothing would give me greater pleasure. . . .'

'You were in Syria in the autumn; I'm surprised that you wouldn't prefer to return to some part of the Middle East which hasn't been spoiled by modernisation. There must be areas remaining which you could reach without too much difficulty.'

'Of course, that *would* be lovely. Bring the wheel round full circle. The Villes Mortes, for instance, wouldn't give much trouble. The area is quite small and you go up to the edge by lorry. It's quite simple to find a man to go with you and horses . . . spend a week there among the ruined basilicas . . . Qalb Lozé, Ruwaiha, Qalat – places like that. Afterwards, I might go down south to the desert and visit the wicked old sheikh who kept me waiting until two in the morning for my dinner! I've not been there since we made the film of the Euphrates raft, four or five years ago. Yes . . . I would like to go back. . . .'

'Last autumn,' I said, 'did you find much change in Damascus and Aleppo?'

'I'm afraid so. Damascus is getting more and more modern buildings – skyscrapers, big hotels . . . more cars in the streets. Aleppo hasn't suffered as much until recently, but it's going the same way . . . you can see all that happening. The day after I left Damascus, a bomb blew away the corner of my hotel . . . narrow squeak. We didn't have any trouble apart from that, however.' She stopped suddenly. 'Did I ever describe to you the houses of Aleppo? They're marvellous. You climb on to the roof of one and go for miles from rooftop to rooftop without ever having to descend into the streets. The roofs have everything: gardens, flowers, vegetables, even donkeys. In hot weather, of course, they sleep up there. . . . You'd be quite safe, off the streets, if any trouble started. Anyhow, trouble doesn't bother me in the least: I'm nearly ninety and I've had a good, long life. They might drop a little bomb in the morning or fire a few shots . . . never lasts long! My work is done – well, very nearly done. Our various books and the final volumes of *Letters* will see the last of it.'

'Quite frankly I'll believe that when it happens! Who's to say you won't begin writing again? You must have enough material for another collection of essays, for example.'

'No, really, I mean it. I'm glad not to have to do it any more . . . don't want the trouble of it. Might begin something else, but I don't honestly think so. It's been interesting for me to work on the photograph book; seeing my whole life go by in pictures . . . such a lot of pictures! That's been fun. . . . Don't forget, sometime you must tell me what you think about my poetry. We might try to plan a book of the scraps; perhaps mix poems together with some of my drawings and make a little volume for amusement. That would be a pleasant conclusion to fifty years involved with literature. There are the Wavell letters also: I've got about twenty, and an old friend has about the same number again. With the replies, and a few words of introduction, there would be another tiny volume; a personal footnote to the life of a great soldier.'

'It seems as though you're very far from being done with writing yet! But your next journey . . . that sounds rather undecided.'

'We'll see – *Insh'allah* . . . if Allah wills. I might try to visit the Turkish coast in June: swimming is best then. Next winter, perhaps, Kanchenjunga!' She smiled, rose and gathered up her Kurdish bag and walking-stick from the floor beside her chair. 'We ought to wander down and have some dinner. Be ready for our work tomorrow!'

It was almost dark and I could see the street-lamps shining through the trees. I switched on the stair-light while Freya glanced round the sitting-room. 'Don't think we've left anything lying about,' she said. 'Nothing we're liable to want this evening.' At the head of the stair she turned to me: 'Nice, isn't it, always to be thinking of setting forth. . . ?'